Book Two: Caesar's Sword: Siege of Rome

David Pilling

© David Pilling 2013.

David Pilling has asserted his rights under the Copyright, Design and Patents Act, 1988, to be identified as the author of this work.

This edition published in 2021 by Sharpe Books.

CONTENTS

Prologue
Chapters 1 – 21

… SIEGE OF ROME

Prologue

Abbaye de Rhuys, Brittany, 570 AD

The glory of Britain is dead. News has reached our monastery of a battle fought in the west of the island, not far from the scene of Arthur's great victory at Mount Badon.

On this occasion it has pleased God to allow the Saxons the victory. No less than three British kings were left dead on the field, their blood mingled with that of five thousand British warriors.

The Saxons, they say, attacked at dawn, while the Britons were still wallowing in their beds. In their arrogance and complacency, our kings did not think to post any guards.

Now the whole of western Britain lies open to the invaders. Our crops shall fill pagan bellies. Fire and sword shall consume our undefended towns. Woe to the people! God have mercy on them, who shall now be conquered and enslaved.

My fires are not all burned out. A flicker of life yet courses through these withered veins, and the incompetence of those charged with guarding the land of my birth fills me with as much rage as sorrow.

It is the custom of old men to decry the state of the world as it is now, and to recall with misty-eyed fondness the glories of their youth. I am reluctant to follow the same path, but the fact remains that Britain is degenerate, and her warriors a pale shadow of their forefathers. Would Arthur, my mighty grandsire, have been caught with his breeches down by a pack of yelping Saxons? Would any of his captains, proud Cei or matchless Bedwyr?

Perhaps I pay too much heed to legend. I never knew my grandsire or any of his men. Their bones lie mouldering in the soil of a dozen battlefields. No more shall Arthur's legion ride forth from Caerleon under the dragon banner, to strike terror and a kind of awed respect into Britain's foes.

Nor have I set eyes on Britain since my early childhood, save a glimpse of its green shores across the sea on clear days. My fate was to serve in distant lands under a foreign chief. His name was Flavius Belisarius. The Pillar of the East, as the Romans called him, a man every bit as great as Arthur.

It is the fate of great men to be betrayed. Arthur was betrayed, and so was Belisarius. How I have wept and prayed for their souls. Foolish, helpless, driveling old man that I am, eking out my declining years in this cramped little cell. Of all the afflictions Gods sends to test His creation, old age is the worst.

I can dimly recall a better time. In my mind's eye I see the city of Rome, restored to something like her former grandeur. The Eternal City, ancient capital of the greatest empire the world has ever known.

And yet she is threatened. Her walls encompassed by a hundred and fifty thousand baying Goths, while scarcely a tenth that number of Romans hurl defiance at them from the ramparts.

I see Belisarius, our golden general, snatching a bow from one of his archers and putting an arrow through the gullet of a Gothic chief.

"Courage, Romans!" he cried above the approving roars of his men, "have no fear of these barbarians. Maintain your trust in God, cast your javelins and spears down on their heads, and you shall see them run."

The defence of Rome was his greatest exploit. Who else could have held her against overwhelming numbers of Goths, while the cowardly citizens threatened to stab him in the back at any moment, and his own troops whined and begged to go home?

Who else could have broken my heart so completely? Even now, after the passage of thirty years, the wound has not healed.

I see the general on his white-faced bay, racing across the plain by the banks of the Tiber at the head of his guards. Six times his number of Gothic cavalry stand between us and the gates of Rome.

"That is Belisarius! Kill the bay!"

The cry erupts from pagan throats. They charge. The sky darkens with steel-tipped rain. Spears, arrows and javelins hammer against my shield. We close around the general. He must be protected at all costs. Without him, our army is a rag-bag of mercenaries and conscripts. With him, we are the Roman legions reborn.

My hand closes around the hilt of Caledfwlch: the sword that Arthur held aloft at Mount Badon and buried in Medraut's guts at Camlann. Julius Caesar's sword, also known as The Red Death, forged by the gods on Mount Olympus.

The sword flames into life. The triumphant war-shouts of the enemy turn to fear and dismay. We are among them. Their guttural voices ring in my ears. Their hot blood whets my grandsire's blade.

Better times. I shall take a little wine, and then take up my pen again to write of Belisarius' greatest victory.

My greatest defeat.

1.

It took me three weeks to recover from the fight in the Hippodrome. I had killed Leo, the traitor and ex-charioteer, but he left me with a broken arm and a fractured jaw.

Belisarius had his guards carry from the arena. The crowd was still chanting my name as they laid me on a stretcher. Delirious with pain, I flickered in and out of consciousness, barely aware of my surroundings. The taste of victory was in my mouth, along with the salt tang of blood.

They carried me through the empty streets to a sanatorium not far from Belisarius' house. He could not shelter me in his own house, for that would have been perceived as a deliberate insult to the Empress Theodora. It was public knowledge that she wanted me dead, and had sponsored Leo as her champion. His death at my hands was a serious defeat for her, and one she would thirst to avenge.

Belisarius appreciated the danger I was in. He posted six of his men to watch over me while I recovered. They were Huns, brawny mercenaries from Scythia, and he put his trust in them over our own people. Theodora's influence spread like an ever-expanding net over the city. There were few among the citizens she could not bribe, threaten or manipulate into doing her will.

Towards the end of my recuperation, the general visited me in person. He came at night, hooded and cloaked, and alone.

I woke from an uneasy sleep to find his narrow features staring down at me. Hollow-cheeked and balding, he still looked more like a priest than a soldier, though his wiry, meatless frame possessed enormous strength and skill at arms. The flame of the tallow candle next my bed reflected in the pits of his large, expressive eyes.

"General," I croaked, endeavoring to sit up, but he placed his hand against my chest and gently pressed me back against the pillows.

"Conserve your strength," he said, "you will need it soon enough. Are you mending? How is your arm?"

I cautiously tried to bend my right arm, which until the previous morning had been held straight in a splint. Leo had broken my elbow during the fight in the arena.

The priest at the sanatorium kept the pain at bay by dosing me with alcohol and poppy juice. His potent medicine kept me in a semi-delirious state for days on end, during which time I suffered terrifying hallucinations. Gradually he lessened the dose, and the devils faded from view.

Relief washed over me as I found that I could bend the arm without too much pain, save a dull ache that throbbed up and down the limb, and flex my fingers.

Belisarius smiled. "Good," he said, "the arm will be weak for a while, but nothing is broken beyond repair. Open your mouth."

I obeyed without question, wincing as pain stabbed through my jaw. Leo, may his soul baste in fire in the lowest circle of Hell, had dislocated it with his knee.

Belisarius tilted my face towards the light. "You have lost four teeth," he said, "I saw them on sale outside the gates of the Hippodrome, the day after your triumph. You are something of a hero among the people, Britannicus Minor."

I winced again. Britannicus Minor was Theodora's mocking pet name for me, bestowed when I was a youth training to be a charioteer in the Hippodrome, and she a common dancer and prostitute. I hated it, but the name became popular when I started racing in the arena.

My mind was still clouded with the lingering effect of opium, and it hurt to form words. "A dead hero, sir," I mumbled, "if I stay in the city."

Belisarius' long face was naturally suited to looking grave. He nodded somberly and lowered his bony rump onto the stool beside my bed.

"My guards have already slain two of Theodora's assassins," he said, "they grow bolder every day. One of them posed as a seller of rare herbs and medicines. He might have passed through if my men hadn't insisted on searching his basket and found the knife. Sooner or later they will abandon stratagems and resort to force. The Empress has only stayed her hand this long for fear of public disgrace. Her husband disapproves of her actions, and has asked her to abandon this ridiculous feud against you."

It seemed incredible that I, a mere ex-charioteer and not very distinguished soldier, should have incurred the wrath of the most powerful woman on earth. But then I knew Theodora of old. For all her outward majesty, she was a vengeful, petty-minded soul, and not one to forgive a slight.

She was also forceful and possessed of a mighty strength of will, far more so than her affable, pleasure-loving husband. Justinian might upbraid her in public, but in private she would work on him until he either went mad or yielded to her desires.

"Fortunately, an easy answer presents itself," Belisarius went on, "our victory in North Africa has given the Emperor a taste for conquest. Italy is next."

I could scarcely believe my ears. The African campaign had been a desperate gamble, and might easily have ended in the total destruction of the Roman army.

Thanks to the favour of God, and the skill of Belisarius, a most unlikely triumph had been achieved. The barbarian Vandals were destroyed in two great battles, their mad king taken prisoner, and the old Roman province returned to imperial rule.

My harrowing experiences on that campaign are burned into my memory. I had fought at Ad Decimum, witnessed the slaughter of the Vandal nation at Tricamarum, and shivered my way through months of siege on Mount Papua. Somehow I survived the ordeal with a reasonably whole skin, though I used up most of my life's supply of good fortune in doing so.

"Madness," I croaked, reaching for the jug of watered wine, "Italy was lost a hundred years ago, and cannot be regained. Caesar should be content with what he has."

Belisarius frowned in disapproval. I noticed the deep lines at the corners of his eyes, and the prominent tendons in his slender neck. We were of an age, both in our middle thirties, but he looked twenty years older.

"It is not for us to question the will of the Emperor," he said severely, "only to do his bidding. This new campaign has come at a good time for you. I shall commission you as an officer in my guards, and take you to Italy with me."

I gaped at him, wondering if the damned priest had drugged my wine.

"It is your only chance," he went on, "my guards cannot protect you forever. It is only by the grace of God that you have evaded Theodora's assassins for so long. You must come with me on this campaign, or die."

Belisarius was risking much on my behalf. I was aware that little love existed between him and Theodora, though his wife, Antonina, enjoyed the Empress's confidence.

Antonina was another who had tried to ensnare me. Belisarius was entirely in her power. To go against her, as well as braving the wrath of Theodora, could only mean he valued me far more than I deserved.

I was in no position to refuse, even if the invasion of Italy was a suicidal venture. The ancient Roman homeland had been in the hands of barbarian Goths and Ostrogoths for over a century, ever since Alaric swept through the country and put Rome herself to the sack. The Gothic peoples were far more numerous and powerful than the Vandals, and their fighting strength could not be exhausted in a couple of pitched battles.

An image passed through my fevered mind of Justinian plucking men from a sack and laughing insanely as he threw them into the maw of a ravenous lion.

Belisarius read the doubts on my face. "I know," he said, "it sounds like death. But the Emperor is no fool. You must trust in his judgment, and mine."

I struggled up onto my good elbow. "I have no choice," I replied, and drained the last of the wine.

The general patted my knee. His wintry face cracked into a grin.

"None," he agreed.

2.

While I lay in a drug-induced fog in the sanatorium, the Gothic rulers of Italy were doing their best to slaughter each other and provide Justinian with a plausible reason to declare war.

The Goths may have been barbarians, yet another strain of the Germanic peoples that overwhelmed the Western Empire, but had quickly acquired civilized Roman habits. In terms of ruthless infighting and dirty politics, Rome had little to teach them.

Let me try and summarise the rat's nest of Gothic politics as best I may.

At this time their queen, Amalasontha, was locked in a vicious power-struggle with Theodatus, nephew of the great Gothic king, Theoderic.

Amalasontha was as proud, cruel and ambitious as any Roman Empress. Her son had died young, debauched to death after a reign of just eight years. Determined to keep her grip on power, but unable to rule alone - the Goths had a horror of being ruled by women - she proposed that she and Theodatus be crowned as joint sovereigns of Italy.

This Theodatus was an old man, renowned, like the Emperor Claudius, for his love of learning and not much else. Amalasontha flattered herself that she had made a cunning choice. Once he was crowned, the old fool could be safely ignored, and she would be the ruler of Italy in fact if not in name.

Alas, she miscalculated. The old fool was not so foolish as all that. Having submitted to her every condition and sworn every oath she demanded of him, Theodatus suddenly pounced and had Amalasontha's servants massacred. The queen herself was arrested and banished to a distant island. There, in the spring of the year 535, she was strangled in her bath by one of her colleague's assassins.

The murder of Amalasontha gave Justinian the perfect excuse to invade. Donning a mask of outrage and indignation, he declared Theodatus a tyrant without legitimate authority, and that Italy must be liberated from his illegal rule.

No further pretext for war was needed. The citizens of Constantinople, their pride and patriotism inflated beyond measure by the easy conquest of Africa, were eager for another taste of military glory.

How I despised them. The fickleness, the cowardice, the sheer arrant stupidity of the Roman mob was the bane of the Empire. They had almost destroyed the city during the Nika riots, and even the bloody vengeance inflicted by Belisarius' veterans had failed to knock some sense into them. They would cheer a man one day and tear him in pieces the next. Now, skillfully manipulated by the Emperor's propaganda, they willingly scraped together the money to help fund another war.

Not that Justinian was short of money. The booty from the North African campaign had filled his coffers to overflowing. Some of the treasure went towards the completion of his pet project, the construction of the gigantic domed cathedral in the heart of Constantinople. The rest was poured into the effort of re-fitting the fleet and raising two new armies.

When I was fit to walk, my guards hurried me out of the sanatorium under cover of darkness, to Belisarius' house. I needed a stick to remain upright, and laboured along the cobbled street like an old man, panting for breath. The Huns grumbled and cursed me in their savage tongue, and in the end two of them seized my arms and half-carried me down the alleyway beside the outer wall of Belisarius' dwelling.

A slave admitted us via the postern gate, and led us across silent, torch-lit gardens towards an arched doorway. Lights blazed in the windows of the ground floor. The door opened onto the narrow vestibule, and beyond that lay the atrium, a large, open central court with a circular pool in the middle.

We followed the gravel path around the pool, towards the double doors at the northern end. These were guarded by two of Belisarius' Veterans, hard-looking men in scale armour, armed with round shields and long spears. They glanced at us suspiciously, but did nothing as the slave pushed open the doors and beckoned us through.

Inside was a large, rectangular chamber with a high roof and a beautifully inlaid mosaic floor. It was a warm night in early spring, so there was no fire laid in the great stone hearth. Three arched and colonnaded doorways led off to other parts of the house, but all my attention was fixed on the three men seated on couches in the middle of the room.

One of the men was Belisarius. As ever, he looked uncomfortable out of military uniform, and his loose robes and fringed mantle hung awkwardly from his tall, bony frame.

His companion to his left was Mundus, the hulking German mercenary and magister militum of all the Roman forces in Illyria and along the Danubian frontier. I had last seen him during the Nika riots, when he led four hundred Huns to slaughter ten thousand Roman citizens. It was impossible to imagine the brute in civilian dress, and despite the heat he was decked out in his usual furs and leathers.

The presence of these two powerful men was intimidating enough, but the third surprised and frightened me.

"Good evening, Coel," said Narses, his ugly face stretched into a smile, "you are fully recovered, I hope. Hardy barbarian stock, eh?"

He was not a welcome or pleasant sight. The last time I was summoned into the presence of Narses and Belisarius, they had coerced me into accompanying the Roman expedition to North

Africa, so I could help steal Caledfwlch from Gelimer, the mad King of the Vandals.

After my return to Constantinople, Narses had rescued me from being boiled alive by Theodora's assassins. I should have felt grateful to him for that, but he was a skilled and subtle politico, and not the sort to do anything except for his own profit. By saving me he offended and humiliated the Empress, and thus reduced her influence.

He was dwarfish little monstrosity, hardly bigger than a child, limping his way through life on a pair of twisted legs. God had seen fit to bring Narses only half-formed into the world. His physical afflictions were offset by an agile brain and burning ambition, and he had risen high in the world through sheer force of will and intellect. Anyone who judged the dwarf on his feeble appearance did so at their peril.

"My lords," I said, with a stilted bow.

The three men had been sitting in silence when we entered, and the air fairly crackled with the tension between them. Belisarius and Mundus were allies and friends, of a sort, but both distrusted Narses. For good reason: the eunuch once cheerfully informed me that anyone who trusted him was a fool, and deserved an early grave.

For all his ugliness, Narses had acquired a certain degree of practiced charm. He rose, or rather dropped, from his seat, and patted the cushion next to his, inviting me to sit.

"Dismissed," growled Mundus, waving away the Huns. They stamped their feet, turned smartly and marched outside. The slave closed the doors behind them and melted into the shadows.

"Wine for the champion of the arena," said Narses, waddling over to the low table beside his couch, "wine for the latest hero of Rome."

Embarrassed, I limped over to the couch and sat, while Narses poured out a rich, red flow from an elegantly fluted silver jug. He handed me the cup and regarded me with something like affection.

"You did splendidly in the arena," he said, "Theodora's face was sheer artistry for days afterwards. I have seldom seen her so enraged."

He sighed happily. "Bliss to behold, I assure you, though I doubt her servants would agree. Their lives have been hell, ever since you plunged your magic sword into Leo's heart."

In truth Leo had fallen onto the blade, but now was not the time to quibble. "I am sorry for that," I replied cautiously, "I never meant to cause any suffering. I have never done anything save follow my conscience."

Belisarius had been watching me closely. "No man who listens to his conscience can thrive for long in this city," he said, "it is a pit of snakes. The sooner we are gone, the better."

Narses smiled indulgently. "Our famous general is too good for politics," he said, winking at me, "in his world, honest men with swords defend the frontiers of the Empire, while corrupt eunuchs and former prostitutes do their best to undermine the state from within. Where is your wife tonight, Flavius?"

Belisarius' jaw tightened. He clearly despised Narses, but for some unfathomable reason had invited the eunuch to his house.

"You know very well," he replied, with forced patience, "Antonina was summoned to the palace tonight."

"As she is most nights. Antonina and Theodora hatch plots together in the Empress's private quarters, while we do the same here. Does the Emperor plot, I wonder? And if so, with whom?"

Mundus shifted impatiently. "I came here to talk of the war," he grunted, "not to chop words and exchange clever insults. I see no reason why we could not have met in open council during the day, instead of creeping about like a pack of thieves in the dark."

"He is the reason," said Narses, pointing at me, "and that pig-sticker he carries."

I touched the hilt of Caledfwlch, which I had strapped on before leaving the sanatorium. Having gone to such lengths to retrieve my grandsire's sword, I never let it out of my sight.

"Show us the sword, Coel," ordered Belisarius. He spoke with the voice of stern authority, and almost without thinking I drew Caledfwlch from its sheath.

Mundus lent forward and squinted at the blade as I held it up to the light. "I see an old-fashioned gladius," he said, "with two golden eagles stamped in the hilt."

"Caesar's sword," Narses explained, "wielded by old Julius himself, and said to have been forged by Vulcan himself in the depths of Mount Olympus. Lost in the mists of Albion for centuries, until it fell into the hands of Coel's ancestor. Some grubby warlord or other."

He hesitated, snapping his fingers and pretending that he had forgotten my grandsire's name. The eunuch loved to play-act and provoke others. Once, I might have fallen for the bait, but was too canny to snap at it now.

"Arthur," I said calmly, taking a long swallow of the excellent wine, "his name was Arthur."

"Just so," said Narses, smiling sweetly at me, "not just any sword, but a symbol and an icon of rare power. Gelimer would have used it to unite the barbarian nations of the world under his banner and destroy the Empire. It must never fall into the wrong hands."

He held out his right hand, palm upwards. "Give it to me."

I slammed Caledfwlch back into its sheath. "Never. That is one order I cannot obey. I will die first."

"Coel speaks the truth," said Belisarius, "I tried to persuade him to give it up in Carthage. He refused. The sword is part of him."

Narses responded to defeats by pretending they hadn't happened. "I merely tested you, Coel," he said, lowering his hand, "you are every bit as brave and honest as I feared. But you must not stay in Constantinople. Your enemies multiply."

He snapped his fingers, and a slave emerged from a shadowy corner, carrying a dark blue woolen cloak scarce big enough to fit a child. He draped it over Narses' lumpen shoulders.

"I take my leave," said the eunuch, "thank you for your hospitality, Flavius. An excellent supper. I must return the favour sometime."

"I look forward to it," Belisarius replied without a hint of sincerity. He and Mundus rose and bowed respectfully as Narses limped out of the room, followed by his slave.

When the doors had closed, Belisarius subsided gratefully onto his couch and stretched out his long legs. All the strain and tension in the air dissolved.

"Thank God for that," he groaned, passing a hand over his face, "if the little swine had stayed much longer, I might have thrown him out of the window."

"Why did he come, anyway?" demanded Mundus, "he talked of nothing but trivialities over supper. Every time I mentioned Italy, he changed the subject."

Belisarius nodded at me. "Narses used our tame Briton to humiliate Theodora, but not had seen him since he was carried from the arena. I made sure of that. He wanted to know if Coel was still alive and whole, and if he could still be used. Now he knows."

Mundus's little eyes raked over me. "Your enemies multiply, Briton," he said, "Narses referred to himself. You should have given him the sword."

"It is mine, sir," I said defensively, "all I have in the world. Without Caledfwlch I am nothing."

"Narses will take it from you, if he can," said Belisarius, "I know that scheming little imp. He craves power, spends every waking hour thinking of ways to obtain it. With Caesar's sword in his hand, there would be no limit to his ambition. Can you imagine him perched on the throne?"

For the first time in weeks I laughed. The effort hurt my jaw, but I was glad of something to lift the clouds gathering over my head.

Belisarius and Mundus spent the next hour discussing the war. I listened avidly.

Justinian had hatched a plan whereby the Romans would attack Italy on two fronts. Mundus would lead the army west and invade Dalmatia, which was held by the Goths, hoping to leech the strength of the enemy by forcing them to defend their eastern province. Meanwhile Belisarius and the Roman fleet would sail south-west, officially to reinforce the Roman garrisons in Africa, but in fact to seize the island of Sicily.

"Sicily will be our stepping-stone to the Italian mainland," said Belisarius, "our forces shall be likened unto a spear, thrust into her soft underbelly."

He grinned at my expression. "Well, that is how the Emperor put it. He is something of a poet, and can turn a decent phrase on occasion."

"What do you make of our plan?" he asked, again watching me closely. I seemed to fascinate these Romans, who regarded me as a relic from some distant world. Their forefathers had lost control of Britain generations ago, and I sometimes wondered if my presence served as a reminder – not always a welcome one – of the diminished Empire's glorious past.

I pondered before answering. By now I was well into my third cup of wine, but even the heady glow of alcohol failed to fill me with optimism.

"If you can conquer North Africa with a mere fifteen thousand men, sir," I said carefully, "then you can certainly repeat the feat elsewhere."

"A shame, then," said Belisarius, "that I won't have fifteen thousand men. The Emperor has given me no more than twelve thousand for the task. Four thousand foederati troops, three thousand Isaurians, some Hunnish and Moorish cavalry, and my bucelarii."

My spirits sank. How many warriors could the King of the Goths muster – forty, fifty thousand? And he could call on the support of his kin in Frankia, Hispania and Germania. If I was of a paranoid disposition, I might have suspected the Emperor of deliberately sending Belisarius to his death.

Yet my only chance of survival was to accompany this suicide mission. With the likes of Narses and Theodora for enemies, my life in Constantinople was not worth a straw.

"Twelve thousand men," I said, "and one Briton."

3.

It took months to re-assemble the imperial fleet, and muster armies for the invasion of Dalmatia and Sicily. Spring passed into summer, and all that time I was kept under guard at Belisarius' house. He had taken a great risk in moving me from the sanatorium, and only done so because I was no longer safe there.

"Not even Theodora's assassins," he assured me, "would think of trying to force entry into my house. Not, at least, while I stand high in the favour of the Emperor."

That favour depended on continued military success. Justinian was a fickle creature, and susceptible to the whispered asides of his courtiers. He was already envious of his general's exploits in Syria and Africa, and for a time entertained suspicions that Belisarius meant to sever ties with the Empire and declare himself King of an independent African province. Only Belisarius' speed in returning to Constantinople and protesting his innocence had cleared him of the taint of treason.

For now, with the laurels of recent victories still fresh on his brow, Belisarius was all but untouchable. Even so, he was not fool enough to presume on his current popularity, and made efforts to deter Theodora's agents. The six Huns who protected me during my convalescence remained at their posts at the sanatorium, guarding an empty room. Meanwhile I was ordered to remain indoors at all times in his house.

This suited me for the time, for I was still weak from my injuries. Belisarius treated me well, and I enjoyed the best of rations from his kitchen. He employed a master-at-arms to spar with me, until my confidence returned and my right arm had regained its strength.

The general himself was often absent, either at the palace or overseeing preparations for war. As before the African campaign, he was drilling his troops on the plains outside the city walls, while the fleet that carried us home was being refitted in the harbour of the Golden Horn.

A similar number of ships were needed to take the army to Sicily, transports and dromons for the most part, along with a few galleys. I pictured the feverish bustle of activity in the harbour, hundreds of hired Egyptian and Syrian sailors and engineers toiling in the summer sun, and groaned at the prospect of another sea-voyage. I was a wretched sailor, a martyr to seasickness, and had barely survived the journey to Africa.

The long days of rest and inactivity did nothing to ease my mind. Fears gnawed at me in the evenings, when shadows crept slowly through the gaps of the shuttered windows and oiled into my bedchamber. I was acutely aware that only the friendship of Belisarius stood between me and destruction. He was an honourable man, but had his weaknesses, chiefly his slavish adoration of Antonina.

Antonina had tried to seduce me in Carthage, as part of a foul plot to disgrace me in the eyes of her husband. I resisted her, but had lived in terror since that she might feed some twisted version of the incident to Belisarius, claiming that I had tried to force myself on her. So far that particular axe had not fallen, but remained suspended over my neck.

I sat and sweated in the growing darkness. Caledfwlch was my only comfort. I often hugged the blade to my chest, as though willing its hard-forged steel into my quaking soul. Sometimes I thought I could hear the screams of all its victims down the centuries, and pictured the hell of Mount Badon, where my grandsire personally laid low hundreds of Saxons in a single charge.

My ordeal ended in the dying days of summer. Belisarius came to his house one evening, exhausted from his labours, and announced that the expedition was ready to sail.

"Mundus has departed for Dalmatia," he said over supper, "along with his son Maurice and ten thousand men. Their object is the Gothic capital, Salona."

He swallowed some wine and dabbed his lips with a cloth. "God grant that Theodatus is as stupid as he seems," he added, "and sends the largest portion of his forces to relieve Salona. Then Italy will be ripe for the taking."

Our best hope of victory lay in the folly of Theodatus, whose wisdom did not extend beyond his academic studies. His murder of Amalasontha was the act of a savage and a political child, for it gave Rome the perfect excuse to try and retake her homeland.

The odds were still stacked against us. Despite his outward confidence, Belisarius was well aware of that. Already old before his time, he seemed to age before my eyes, and I started to fear for his health. If he broke down or even – God forbid! – died, there was no-one to protect me.

By the beginning of autumn, all was ready. My gentle confinement finally came to an end, and I was smuggled out of Belisarius' house one moonless night with the same Hunnish escort that had brought me there. The seven of us, muffled up in dark hoods and cloaks, hurried down to the docks, where a boat was waiting to row me out to Belisarius' flagship.

If there were spies watching us from the shadows, none tried to impede our progress. The Huns were armed with swords and braces of knives under their cloaks, and I had Caledfwlch, so it would have gone hard for any that tried.

The harbour was relatively quiet, with just a few groups of weary Egyptian sailors stockpiling bales of fodder and other supplies ready to be carried out to the fleet. They paid no heed to us, or the troop of soldiers with torches waiting for us at a jetty.

A tall, bareheaded man stood among the mailed and helmed soldiers. We had never spoken, but I recognized him instantly as he stepped forward to greet me.

His name is famous now, but at this time Procopius of Caesarea was still a young man, and relatively unknown. A Jewish scholar and historian, he had acted as Belisarius' legal advisor, secretary and general confidante on the African campaign. He was no soldier, but did not lack for courage, and had undertaken several dangerous missions on the general's behalf.

In person he was of medium height, and always put me in mind of a starving bird of prey. His body was lean, with long arms and legs, and his oversized head was stuck on the end of a scrawny neck. Prominent cheekbones, slightly protruding eyes, thin lips and a long, hooked nose completed the effect.

"Hurry, he whispered, casting anxious glances over my shoulder, "before the wolves that tracked you here find the courage to strike."

"I saw no-one," I said as the Huns bundled me down the ladder into the boat. He sniffed and folded his arms tight against his skinny chest.

"Of course you didn't," he muttered, his big eyes narrowing to slits as he peered into the darkness, "the Empress employs professionals. You wouldn't know they were near until you felt steel in your back."

The waters were calm, but the boat rocked alarmingly when my foot slipped on the lowest rung. I dropped into it like a stone and incurred the displeasure of the oarsman, who cursed me for a handless idiot.

"Quiet, you fools!" hissed Procopius, "do you want the entire city to hear? Perhaps we should bang a gong, or sing a few hymns?"

He hitched up his robe and made his way awkwardly down the ladder, exposing a good deal of pale thigh. His descent into the boat was scarcely less clumsy than mine, but the oarsman evidently knew better than to curse Belisarius' private secretary. Biting his lip, he poled us out into the harbour.

Procopius hunkered down in the stern, and sat eyeing me with cool interest. "Coel ap Amhar," he said, with a decent stab at British pronunciation, "I have watched your progress for some time now. The refugee who became a slave, who became a charioteer, who became a soldier. Equally at home in the Hippodrome, or the camp of the Heruli, or the imperial court."

He rested his chin on his fist. "Your face is a blank canvas. Any number of personas can be painted on it and wiped clean, ready for the next. A play-actor."

I bridled at that. "I am nothing of the sort," I replied, careful to keep my voice low, "and have never pretended to be anything I am not. I do what is necessary to survive."

"Of course. As we all do. But a great deal is necessary in order to survive in Constantinople. You have made your way in the city for over thirty years. From the gutter to an officer in Belisarius' personal guard. Quite a tale."

My pride gave a flicker. "I am still in the gutter," I said, "you know my name, but not my quality. I am Coel ap Amhar ap Arthur, grandson of the First Warlord of the Island of the Mighty, descendent of the ancient line of British princes and kings. The blood of Coel Hen, ruler of the North, grandsire of Constantine the Great, runs in my veins."

Procopius rubbed his thin hands and gave an enigmatic smile. "Belisarius told me you were proud. I suppose a man with nothing save his name and an old sword must cleave to pride. Step carefully, Coel, and be wary lest you fall further."

He said nothing more, but lapsed into a brooding silence as the boat sculled across the dark waters to the looming bulk of Belisarius' flagship.

This was the largest galley in the fleet, and one of the few old-fashioned Roman warships still in use. It was of the type called a bireme, with two staggered banks of oars and a long, narrow prow. Biremes were usually propelled by oars, with just a single sail, but this had been converted into a three-mast vessel. Unlike the lumbering transports and the smaller dromons, the galley had a sleek, dangerous look, and resembled some kind of dormant sea-monster as she lay resting at anchor inside the harbour.

We drew alongside, and a rope-ladder was let down the side. I was the first up, helped aboard by two brawny Sicilians.

I half-expected Belisarius to be there to greet me, but doubtless the general had more pressing matters to attend to. The ship's captain, a heavy-set Greek with a long pink scar running from his temple to his jaw, regarded me with impatience.

"You're to get below," he said, jerking his thumb at the hatchway leading to the bowels of the ship, "and stay there until sent for. Quickly, if you please. I haven't slept for two bloody days, and there is still much to do."

I obeyed, and clambered down the ladder into the damp, musty-smelling space below deck. Even though the ship lay at anchor in peaceful waters, her gentle motion was enough to make my guts churn a little. The smell of tar and the salt tang of the sea in my nostrils brought back memories of the nightmarish voyage to Africa.

Procopius followed me down the ladder. "I am also a poor sailor," he said, noting my pained expression, "but with luck our voyage shall be a short one."

"Why do I have to hide down here?" I demanded, trying to ignore the thought of being cooped up below deck in a pool of my own vomit when the fleet sailed for Sicily.

"Your enemies may or may not know where you are," he replied, "I have little doubt you were followed from Belisarius' house, but the agents of Narses and Theodora cannot touch you here, aboard the general's own flagship. This is his territory. Any violation of it would be perceived as a direct insult to Belisarius. Whatever petty grudges and feuds that may exist, Rome cannot afford to alienate its greatest soldier."

He pursed his thin lips and leaned against a bulkhead. "For now, at any rate. If Belisarius fails in Italy, he will be dead or disgraced, and you will be fair game."

I had discerned as much, and was anxious to get away from Constantinople as far and as swiftly as possible. "When does the fleet put to sea?" I asked.

"Tomorrow, if all goes to plan. Mundus is already laying siege to Salona, and Belisarius can afford no delay."

A few more hours, then, and I would be safe. "What if Theodora and Narses send agents after me? No-one would notice a few men disguised as soldiers."

"Perhaps. Theodora, at least, has no need for such crude stratagems. Her greatest agent will be among us, in plain view."

It took me a moment to fathom his meaning. "Yes," he said, reacting to the horror on my face, "Antonina is coming with us."

4.

The fleet put to sea the next morning, propelled down the straits of the Bosphorus by a fair wind and the cheers of the multitude gathered on the docks. Their cheers were mingled with the dirge-like chants of the priests, clashing cymbals, screeching trumpets, and the tolling of every church bell in the city.

Before the African expedition, the Emperor and the Patriarch came to the harbour in person to give the fleet their blessing. They did so again now, though the Patriarch was so old he had to be carried in a litter. I heard the roar of the crowd treble in volume as Justinian arrived, preceded by the droning of bull-horns and escorted by six hundred of his personal guard, the Excubitors.

Heard, but did not see. I was confined below deck with two Huns to protect me and ensure I stayed hidden. They were a couple of surly, yellow-skinned brutes, typical of their race, and dripping with weaponry.

"No need to watch me so closely, boys," I said with feigned cheerfulness, "I'm quite happy where I am."

At last the moment I dreaded arrived. The ship began to move. I crouched in a corner, draping my cloak over me as a blanket and preparing for the worst.

The histories will tell you that the Roman fleet encountered no difficulty on the short voyage from Constantinople to Sicily. No storms delayed our progress, the winds were constant, and the Sicilian coast completely undefended. The Emperor's ruse had worked. The Gothic fleet, such as it was, had sailed north carrying troops and supplies to reinforce their garrisons in Dalmatia.

To me, trapped below deck in the grip of sea-sickness, the voyage was a miserable and painful ordeal. The Huns kindly provided me with a bucket, which they emptied at regular intervals. Procopius visited me once or twice, to give me updates and check that I hadn't puked myself to death.

"You are a better sailor than you claimed," I whispered during one of his visits.

Procopius smiled weakly. He was even paler than usual, and trembled slightly, but his illness was nothing compared to mine. I could not walk, or eat, and shivered uncontrollably like a sick dog.

"Courage," he replied, "we will soon be on dry land, and there will an end to this damned creaking and lurching. Belisarius means to land at Catania."

This made sense. Catania was a desolate, rocky stretch of dried lava, near the base of Mount Etna. He had landed there before on the way to North Africa.

"What then?" I asked, drawing my blanket closer around me. My guts gave a sudden heave, and Procopius' answer was delayed while I retched feebly into the bucket.

"We march on Palermo," he said when I was done, "once the principal city falls, the rest of Sicily will follow. An easy conquest."

Too easy, was my initial thought. Even a dotard like Theodatus would surely not have left the island undefended. My suspicious mind spun all kinds of alternatives. Perhaps the Goths were waiting in force at Palermo, to attack our much smaller army as we marched inland. Perhaps their fleet was hidden, somewhere among Sicily's northern coastline, and would emerge to fall upon ours at Catania.

"What of Antonina?" I asked, dragging my mind away from these dreadful scenarios, "does she I know I am aboard?"

"Oh yes. I was with Belisarius when he mentioned your presence to her, two days ago. Our tame Briton, he called you."

I swallowed hard, and rested my head against the hull. "How did she react?"

Procopius shrugged. "She didn't. As far as her husband is aware, you mean nothing to her. She must have known you were aboard anyway."

He squatted down on his haunches. "Attend to me, Coel," he said severely, "for your life is most certainly in danger. Antonina has brought her son, Photius, the fruit of one of her previous marriages."

I blinked at him. The name was vaguely familiar to me, but I had never seen Photius, and knew nothing of him.

"He is very young, barely grown to manhood," Procopius added, "and has inherited his mother's courage and fair looks. There, unless he is a better actor than I judge him to be, the resemblance ends. There is no deceit in him. Rather, he is impulsive, and constantly at Belisarius' elbow, begging him for a command. Eager to win glory at the point of a sword."

"Is he a threat to me?" I asked, who cared nothing for Photius or his ambitions.

"Possibly. He adores his mother, though she appears to care nothing for him. There is little he would not do to win her approval."

"Including murder?"

"I don't know. Perhaps. Antonina would not hesitate to use him as a weapon against you. The question is whether he would agree to it."

Procopius thought for a moment, tapping his finger-tips together. "I think," he said eventually, "that Belisarius should give this valiant young man a chance to prove himself."

His eyes bored into mine. "Yes. Photius should be among the first to be sent ashore. Perhaps he can be dispatched on a scouting mission inland, with just a few men for company. Picked men."

I knew what Procopius was implying. It filled me with revulsion, but I was too old and battle-hardened to be entirely scrupulous.

"You would go to such lengths, for me?" I asked quietly, "why?"

"Belisarius values you, as an officer and a friend," he replied, rising, "he asked me to see you safe. He commands, and I obey. Not that I have any objection to seeing Antonina thwarted. She hates me, as she hates anyone with influence over her husband. She wants Belisarius all to herself."

"Does she love him?"

Procopius gave a dry chuckle, the nearest he ever got to laughter. "Like an epicure loves his dinner. Antonina will eat him alive and then toss away the bones."

I remained below deck until the fleet made landfall at Catania, which lies on the east coast of Sicily, facing the Ionian Sea. Despite the harsh and rugged landscape, there was a city here, much reduced from its former wealth and status after being sacked by the Vandals. The garrison offered no resistance, and opened the city gates to our soldiers after Belisarius promised not to sack the town or molest the inhabitants.

I was sick of concealment, and of languishing in my own stench in the stuffy hold. The Huns were sick of me too, and watched impassively as I crawled feebly up the ladder onto deck.

The sunlight was dazzling, and I had to shade my eyes until they grew used to the unaccustomed glare. I tried to stand on the deck as it gently rose and fell beneath me, but my shaking legs gave way.

A strong hand gripped my forearm as I fell, and hauled me upright. "Steady, old man," said a familiar voice, "we shall have to find you a stick to lean on."

I opened my eyes a crack and gazed on the rugged, dark-skinned features of Bessas, one of Belisarius' chief cavalry officers. He was a Thracian of Gothic origin, fluent in the Gothic language, and I had often overheard him croaking songs in that harsh, guttural language.

Belisarius was a good judge of officers, and could scarcely have chosen a better man to lead his cavalry in Italy. Not only did Bessas speak the language of the enemy, but he was a tough, resourceful veteran of many campaigns, in his mid-fifties or thereabouts, and strong as a bull. His fingers had a grip like steel on my wasted arm. If he had increased the pressure, he might have snapped the bone.

"Coel, isn't it?" he asked after I had mumbled my thanks, "our sickly Briton. God help us, you look like you've puked out your innards. I thought the Britons were a seafaring race?"

"I am the exception," I groaned, clutching my aching belly, "though doomed to spend my life being dragged back and forth across the sea."

Bessas smiled and patted me roughly on the back. "You can go ashore at once, if you like, " he said, "look there."

He pointed at the hundreds of longboats and other smaller vessels that populated the stretch of ocean between our fleet and the coast. The city of Catania was visible to the east, dominated by the brooding shadow of Mount Etna. Procopius had informed me that the volcano last erupted during the days of the Roman Republic, and swamped the greater part of the city in an ocean of boiling lava and hot ash.

Our entire army was disembarking, with a calm order and efficiency that made for a stark contrast to the last time I had witnessed a Roman army disembark, on the north coast of Africa. There all had been chaos and haste, as our sickness-ravaged soldiers struggled to shore in terror of the Vandals falling upon them at any moment.

I spotted Belisarius on the foredeck, standing among a little knot of officers and advisors. Procopius was among them, listening and nodding gravely while the soldiers talked. He was wearing his enigmatic little smile, and I could guess his opinion of what was being said.

Thankfully, there was no sign of Antonina, though a golden-haired young man among the officers might have been Photius. "I was appointed one of the general's personal guard," I said, "my place is by his side."

"Admirable," smirked Bessas, "but you're no use to him in your current state. Go ashore and recuperate. For now, the conquest of Sicily will have to proceed without you."

He gave me back to my Hunnish guards, who had followed me above deck like a couple of faithful hounds, and barked at them to take me ashore. Somehow I found the strength to climb down a rope ladder into one of the launches. I took my place alongside a group of Isaurian archers, and listened in silent misery to their excited chatter as the boat rowed into the shallows.

I could see our army deploying on the broad plain south-west of the city, thousands of tiny doll-figures busily pitching tents and digging temporary fortifications. As usual, Belisarius was taking no chances. The majority of his troops would camp outside the city, along with the baggage, while troops of light horse were sent out to scout the countryside.

Anxious to be rid of boats and sailing, I dropped over the side as soon as it seemed safe, and staggered through warm, waist-deep waters towards the beach. The Huns dogged my steps, which was a comfort. Nobody watching could have any doubt that I was well-guarded, and still enjoyed the favour and protection of Belisarius.

From Catania the army marched north-west, leaving a garrison of two hundred men to hold the city. Belisarius had furnished me with a horse, and I rode at an easy peace in the rearguard, enjoying the peace and beauty of the island. Sicily basked in the autumn sun, and the lengthy, oppressive heat of summer had given way to a pleasant mildness. The hedges on the roadsides were loaded with prickly pears. When my stomach had eased, I promptly ruined it again by indulging in too much of the succulent fruit, and afforded the troops much amusement by throwing up in a ditch.

Our army hugged the coast, while the fleet kept in sight to the east, but there was no need for such precautions. As Procopius had predicted, Sicily was an easy conquest, and we encountered no resistance on the march to Palermo. The native farmers presented us with gifts of bread and fruit, and expressed warm enthusiasm at being rescued from the tyranny of the Goths.

Some tyranny, I remember thinking as I looked around at the prosperous little villages and fertile, well-tilled farmland. The Sicilians had no cause to hate their occupiers.

"They might soon have cause to hate us," remarked Procopius when he rode down the line to speak with me, "if we are defeated in Italy, the Goths will exact a bloody revenge for their treachery. If we are victorious, and the island remains part of the Empire, the Emperor will squeeze them for everything they have. Sicily produces abundant crops of grain. Justinian will take it all in annual tribute, leaving the inhabitants to live on grass."

Palermo was approached from the south via a road winding through craggy mountains. Belisarius sent horsemen ahead to scout the route. I saw Photius among them, his fair hair gleaming like burnished gold as he galloped at the head of a troop of Herulii. They returned unscathed – Procopius had had no opportunity to put his murderous little plan into effect – to report that the road was unguarded.

The city was an astonishingly beautiful sight, its whitewashed walls gleaming like pale diamond. I first saw it from a ridge overlooking the bay. Blue mountains enclosed and concealed Palermo from the landward side, and the sea from the east. I shaded my eyes and glimpsed the first of our ships rounding the headland to the south.

I also saw that the harbour was undefended. The garrison had closed the gates against us, but the city was open to assault from land and sea. There was no Gothic army lying in wait, hidden among the mountains. Either deliberately or through sheer negligence, Theodatus had left Sicily to its fate.

Keen to score a bloodless victory, Belisarius sent forward messengers to demand Palermo's surrender. The garrison sent back a haughty reply, ordering the Romans to withdraw from their walls or face destruction.

That night Belisarius summoned his officers to a council of war. My presence was also required, along with five other members of his personal guard. I struggled into my heavy chain mail and crested helmet, and limped down to the general's pavilion.

"I will not waste time in a siege," said Belisarius, thumping his fist on the table set up in the middle of his tent. A map of Sicily rested on the table, with various lead markers representing our forces.

Bessas was present, along with Constantine and Valentinian, the general's two other chief officers, and Galierus, the admiral of the fleet. Procopius was there in his capacity as secretary. He briefly glanced up at me as I came in, and then sidelong at Photius.

Seen at close quarters, Antonina's son had something of the Greek god about him. Tall and blonde, well-made and impossibly handsome in a sculpted sort of way, he seemed to glow with a strange inner light, putting the rest of us in the shade. All his attention was on Belisarius, and he paid me no heed whatsoever.

"Then we must take the city by storm," said Bessas, leaning over to study the map, "I suggest an attack at dawn from east and west. The Gothic garrison will be spread thin to repel us. Bloody work, but it can be done."

There was a murmur of agreement from Constantine and Valentinian. Like him, they were a couple of hard-faced veterans. The three of them put me in mind of a pack of old mastiffs.

Steel flashed in the gloom of the tent. Photius had drawn his spatha, and slapped it down on the table. "General, I beg the honour of leading the vanguard!" he piped in the high-pitched, breaking voice of adolescence, "I will be the first man up the ladders!"

Procopius smirked, and the officers looked unimpressed, but Belisarius regarded him fondly. "I think not, brave Photius," he said gently, "your mother would nail my skin to the walls of Palermo if any harm befell you."

The boy's flawless skin flushed with angry blood, and his lower lip trembled. He looked on the verge of hysterics, but Belisarius lifted a hand to calm him.

"Peace," he said patiently, "you will have a chance to show your valour. Not, however, in the vanguard. That is not the place for untried youths."

Mention of Antonina made my skin prickle. I had glimpsed her a few times on the march, in a covered litter toward the rear of the army, lying full-length on a comfortable divan and sunning herself with the silk curtains drawn back. She had brought her ladies with her. At Palermo Belisarius set up a little camp for them apart from the main army, well away from the prying eyes and lustful impulses of our soldiers. I had heard rumours that she insisted on being present at her husband's military councils, and even on giving him advice, but tonight she kept her distance.

Belisarius switched his attention to Galierus. "How deep are the waters of the bay?" he asked, "deep enough for our ships to approach within bow-shot of the walls?"

"Yes, general," the admiral replied.

"Then we shall attack at dawn," Belisarius said cheerfully, "and the city shall fall without a single casualty on our side. What do you think of that, Bessas?"

The old soldier and his colleagues looked nonplussed. "I think it most unlikely, sir," he replied, "the Goths may have been abandoned by their king, but they are determined to resist."

"There must be blood," said Constantine, "and lots of it."

Belisarius burst out laughing. I had rarely seen him in a better humour, and looked questioningly at Procopius, but he ignored me.

"God bless you, you old butchers," said the general, wiping a tear of mirth from his eye, "there must be blood, eh? Well, let it be Gothic blood, for I have no intention of wasting ours on this flyspeck of a city."

His officers looked offended, as well they might, for they were all proud men. Their sullen humour quickly melted to disbelief as Belisarius went on to outline his plan. I listened with mounting admiration for this extraordinary soldier, whom God had sent to rescue the Empire from disgrace and decay.

I spent the night in one of the guard tents close to Belisarius' pavilion. In the morning we were roused early to accompany him onto the high bluffs overlooking Palermo. From there we watched Galierus, who had returned to the fleet after the council, carry out the general's orders.

The bay of Palermo, as I have said, was open and undefended. During the night sixteen of our transports had used their oars to crowd into the harbour, as close to the sea-walls as the depth of water would allow. I could see the steel helmets of the Gothic soldiers on the battlements. They had no catapults or ballistae, and must have had a limited supply of arrows, for they did nothing but watch as our ships rowed closer.

Belisarius had ordered his Isaurian spearmen and archers to assemble in battalions on the plain beyond the eastern walls of the city. Scaling ladders had been fetched from the baggage, and three great battering rams pieced together. To the Goths, it must have looked as though we were preparing for an all-out assault.

It was a ruse. When our ships were within range, their crews used ropes and chains to hoist longboats and other smaller vessels up to the mastheads. Picked archers and javelin-men then clambered up the rigging and jumped into the boats.

Only now did the Goths realise what was afoot. The mastheads of our ships were much higher than the ramparts of the sea-defences. From their lofty height our men now unleashed a hail of arrows and javelins down on the exposed heads of the enemy. Some lit fire-arrows, and shot them into the town itself, where they set roofs and houses aflame and spread terror among the citizens.

"You see?" said Belisarius, nudging Bessas with his elbow, "I said we would take Palermo without losing a drop of Roman blood. We should have had a wager on it."

"The city has not fallen yet," grumbled the other man, but the general was right. The fighting spirit of the Goths was not as stout as their spokesmen had pretended. Even as we watched, the archers on the walls abandoned their posts and fled into the streets, leaving dozens of dead and wounded strewn on the ramparts, their bodies stuck full of missiles.

Panic rippled through the city. A bell sounded inside one of the larger churches, and we saw the tiny figures of the citizens running to and fro. Our archers continued to pour flaming arrows into the streets. More buildings caught fire, especially in the poorest quarters, where all was dry timber and thatch. Plumes of blackish smoke twisted into the sky, while orange flames danced and leaped from one roof to another.

Antonina was present, clothed all in white silk, which lent her the appearance of a goddess among so many rough, ill-favoured soldiers. She clung to her husband's arm, and occasionally leaned in to whisper something in his ear. It angered me to see how he doted on her. All his attention should have been fixed on the battle below, but Antonina distracted him from his duty.

Do I sound envious? Perhaps a little. She was a great beauty, especially in those days, and unlike her friend Theodora required little artifice to sustain that beauty against the advancing armies of time. Her milky complexion remained as fresh as a young girl's, though she was well into her thirties by now. The golden hair, which she wore bound up in the aristocratic Roman style, with long, curly ringlets framing her delicate cheeks, was as lustrous as ever. I feared her, and desired her, and all the time struggled to avert my eyes from her.

Thankfully, she paid no attention to me, or pretended not to. Her son Photius was absent. As a sop to the boy's eagerness, Belisarius had allowed him to join one of the assault-parties mustered on the plain. He was safe enough, for they were destined to see no action.

"Not long now," remarked Procopius, who had shuffled next to me. He was gazing complacently down at the chaos inside Palermo, like a hawk contemplating its prey.

The courage of the Goths soon wilted. Barely two hours after we begun our assault, their gates opened and a group of dignitaries filed out, waving olive branches in a token of peace.

Belisarius agreed to discuss terms. They were straightforward enough: in return for clemency, the Goths agreed to lay down their arms and surrender the city. Belisarius allowed the garrison to march out with honour, unarmed but with their banners flying, and to take ship for the Italian mainland.

With the fall of Palermo, his conquest of Sicily was effectively complete. Leaving a strong garrison to hold the city, he marched south to Syracuse, an ancient city in the south-east corner of the island.

The Gothic governor yielded it up without the faintest show of resistance, and Belisarius entered in triumph at the head of his bucelarii. I rode close behind him. My sickness had passed completely, and my spirits were buoyed by the rapturous reception.

By now our commander's fame had spread to every corner of Sicily. The people of Syracuse flocked to welcome and applaud the conqueror of Africa and hail him as a new Caesar. Belisarius knew how to court popularity, and scattered gold coins and medals among the adoring crowds as he rode through the streets.

My joy was tempered with caution. The chants of *Caesar! Caesar!* were disquieting. Rome already had a Caesar in the form of Justinian, and it wouldn't take much for the Emperor's suspicions of Belisarius to flare hot again. He had his spies among our army. If Belisarius gloried too much in the acclaim of the mob, they would go racing back to Constantinople to pour fresh rumours of treason into Justinian's ears.

Belisarius took up residence in the governor's palace. There he received a steady flow of Gothic officers and diplomats from all over Sicily, come to bend the knee before him and swear allegiance to the Empire.

He took pains to dress in the plain garb of a soldier, and display no signs of arrogance or pretensions above his station. To no avail. The Goths insisted on addressing him in the most servile manner, as though he were indeed the Emperor instead of his representative. One or two even called him Caesar to his face.

I stood beside his chair as the Goths filed into the audience chamber. They were a beautiful people, tall and strongly-made, with auburn hair and fresh, clear-eyed features. The contrast with our swarthy, stunted eastern soldiers was marked, and I sometimes noticed the Goths glancing at us with contempt.

How, I could almost hear them thinking, *have we been conquered by these dwarves?*

It was a question my own ancestors must have asked themselves, after the Roman legions of old had defeated Caradog, the last native British chief in arms, and sent him in chains to Rome.

When business was done for the day, and the last Goth had departed, Belisarius relaxed gratefully in his chair and yawned.

"Wine, in Heaven's name," he croaked, massaging his dry throat. I poured some from a silver jug and handed him the goblet. He downed it one swallow, wiped his lips, and grinned at me.

"Lend me your sword, Coel," he asked, stretching out his hand.

"Come," he said impatiently when I hesitated, "do you think I am going to steal it? I merely wish to hold the thing for a moment."

Reluctantly, I drew Caledfwlch and placed the hilt in his hand. He held the blade vertically before him and gazed at his reflection in the oiled and polished steel.

"I came, I saw, I conquered," he murmured, "but unlike you, Julius, I lost not a single man."

He weighed the sword in his hand, holding it at different angles and examining the eagles stamped into the hilt.

"I thought I might feel something," he said, handing it back to me, "some tingle of power. Foolish. A sword is just a sword, no matter how many illustrious hands have wielded it. A tool for killing people."

"I think otherwise, sir," I said, hurriedly sliding Caledfwlch back into the sheath, "part of my grandsire's soul rests inside this blade. I am certain of that. Perhaps Julius Caesar's as well."

He raised a skeptical eyebrow. "It must be crowded in there. Your belief smacks of paganism, Coel. A man's soul cannot be hacked up like a loaf of bread. It is pure and indivisible."

"Oh God," he added, yawning again and stretching his long limbs, "let us not discuss such weighty matters. I have had a bellyful of them for one day."

Despite his weariness, Belisarius seemed relaxed and cheerful. Sicily had fallen. The crushing weights of duty and responsibility had lifted, however briefly, from his narrow shoulders.

We spent the best part of three months in Sicily, waiting for the arrival of spring and the new campaign season. Belisarius made preparations to invade Italy, while diplomats sped back and forth between Theoderic in Ravenna and Justinian in Constantinople, striving to find some peaceful compromise.

I did remarkably little. The life of a guard officer during peacetime is not a taxing one. When not exercising or on duty, I explored the countryside around Syracuse in the company of Procopius, took care to avoid Antonina and Photius, and was reasonably content. Even in winter, Sicily was a fair island.

"I can picture myself living here," I said to Procopius during one of our idle excursions, "settle down on a little farm with some local woman, hang Caledfwlch above the hearth, and raise goats."

Procopius' mouth twisted in distaste. "You have just described one my images of Hell," he said sourly, "the sooner we can leave this patch of dirt, the better. So far this war has been more akin to a holiday."

"What is wrong with that?" I asked, smiling at him, "if only all wars were so pleasant and straightforward."

"I am a historian, Coel, among other things. My ambition is to witness and record great events, and the deeds of great men. How many pages will my account of the conquest of Sicily fill? One? It will require all my powers of hyperbole and exaggeration to make it worth the reading."

"Then your history is in safe hands," I said cheerfully, giving my reins a shake, "for I never knew a better liar."

The idyll could not last. Word reached us of some disturbance in North Africa, where some of the Moorish desert tribes had revolted against Roman rule. They were inspired by an absurd prophecy, told by one of their female prophets, that they could only be defeated in battle by beardless soldiers. Our generals in Africa all sported beards on their chins, which was enough to persuade the Moors that they could rise up and overthrow our government.

Belisarius dispatched Procopius to Carthage, to talk with the Roman governor and assess the seriousness of the situation. I was sorry to see him go, for the secretary had become something of a friend, but he assured me of a swift return.

"The governor in Carthage is an old woman," he sneered, "else he would have stamped on these Moorish desert-rats as soon as they raised their heads. Belisarius should be wiser in his choice of subordinates."

He was gone for several weeks, during which time I amused myself in a dalliance with a shopkeeper's daughter in Syracuse. She was my first woman since Elene, the Greek dancer who betrayed me, and I am sorry to say that I have only the vaguest memory of her appearance and character. I do recall that her parents had no objection to me staying in her bedchamber on a nightly basis. To the conqueror, as some wise man once said, the spoils.

Procopius did return, but not in the expected manner. He arrived at Syracuse in an open boat, half-dead of thirst, starvation and exposure, with just seven companions, all in an equally wretched state.

One of them, though I nor anyone else crowded into the harbour could believe it, was the governor of North Africa. His name was Solomon, and he stood in the prow of the boat, beating his breast and feebly uttering the same cry, over and over:

"Africa has fallen!"

5.

Belisarius had the seven men taken to the palace on a litter, and there cared for until any danger to their lives had passed. The governor, Solomon, insisted on speaking to Belisarius of the catastrophe that had befallen the Roman province in North Africa.

I accompanied the general to Solomon's bedchamber – I was becoming Belisarius' shadow – and listened to the sick man give his account.

Solomon was proud, far more competent and dutiful than Procopius gave him credit for, and had done his best to hold onto the province. Alas, it would have taken a man of far greater abilities to deal with the fearful catalogue of treason and rebellion that he reported.

"The trouble started with the Moors," he said weakly, "at first it was just a few raids on isolated villages. Nothing out of the ordinary, and I left our local garrisons to cope with them. Then I received word that some of the desert tribes had formed a coalition. They fell upon a detachment of our infantry and cut our soldiers all to pieces."

He paused to cough and drink some water. I glanced at Belisarius. The general's face was as grim as ever I saw it, like a bust carved in stone.

Besides one other guardsman and myself, no-one else was present. The shutters on the bedchamber's single window were closed, blocking out the wintry afternoon sun. Belisarius wanted the details of the African disaster to be kept secret for as long as possible.

"When I heard of the massacre, I resolved to act," Solomon continued, "and led out our garrison in force from Carthage to give battle."

Belisarius gave a slight nod of approval. He would have done no less.

"We met the Moors on a fair open field and utterly routed them. You know what poor soldiers they make. They wear no armour, and their flimsy shields and javelins were no match for Roman arms. I followed up, hoping to destroy the survivors, and found them entrenched in a strong position on Mount Burgaon. I threw in our infantry, and in one assault they cleared the trenches and drove the Moors like sheep, until the desert ran red with their tainted blood."

"So far, a textbook campaign," murmured Belisarius, "what went wrong?"

Solomon laid his head back on the pillows and closed his eyes. "The tribes retreated into the recesses of the desert, where we could not follow," he said, "and then our men started to disintegrate. I did not realise until it was too late, but the army was rotten with sedition. Most of the protestors were Arians. The heresy is still strong in Africa. They complained of Justinian's harsh edits against their faith, and that they were barred from baptizing their children. They complained that the plunder taken from the defeated Moors was not shared out equally. They complained of these and other matters with loud and bitter voices, and the disaffection quickly spread among our orthodox troops. Meanwhile the Moors were allowed to recover their strength."

It was now that Solomon's failure became apparent. As governor and commander-in-chief, he should have stamped down hard on the dissenting voices. Belisarius was of a naturally merciful disposition, but had never hesitated from applying old-fashioned Roman discipline when necessary. I remember the pair of drunken Hunnish confederates he had executed on the hills above Heraclea, and their headless bodies tossed into the sea.

"Unknown to me, some of our garrison troops met at Mount Auras," said Solomon, "and there formed a pact with the Moors and the worst of the Arian dissenters. They raised the standard of revolt against Roman rule. At the same time, a ship bearing four hundred Vandals taken captive in the recent wars was on its way to our eastern provinces. The Vandals were supposed to enlist in our armies there. As the ship sailed past the African coast, the Vandals rose in revolt, slaughtered the sailors and marines, and forced the captain to land. They joined with the rebels at Mount Auras."

He passed a hand over his face. "The Arian poison had even spread to Carthage. Some of the fanatics there plotted against my life, and chose Easter as the best time to murder me. They planned to have me killed as I entered the cathedral before the ceremony. However, when news reached them of the rebel host gathered at Mount Auras, they threw aside all caution and forswore their allegiance to Rome."

Belisarius could contain himself no longer. "And what in the hells were you doing, while all this was going on?" he demanded through gritted teeth.

I had never seen him so angry. His sallow cheeks had turned the colour of fresh steak, and his fists were clenched until the bony knuckles turned white. A thick blue vein throbbed dangerously on his forehead.

"I was planning to march on the rebels, sir," Solomon replied hastily, "but the conspiracy in Carthage took me by surprise. The Arians took to the streets at night. They smashed and plundered the houses of wealthy citizens and slaughtered all in their path, regardless of age, rank or degree. I tried to raise the garrison to sally out against them, but our men were seized with terror, and refused to move. When the mutineers forced the doors of the palace, I was obliged to flee for my life, and take refuge in a chapel. Procopius and a few loyal attendants fled with me. When dawn broke, and the mutineers were drowsy with wine and murder, we crept down to the harbour and stole a boat."

"And so came here," said Belisarius. He pressed his fingertips together and held them to his lips for a moment. I watched him in silence, wondering what even that superb military mind could conceive to reverse such a disaster.

"How many of our ships are ready to sail immediately?" he asked suddenly.

"Just your flagship, sir," I replied, "the rest of our fleet is either being re-fitted, or scattered among the other Sicilian ports."

Just for a second, the briefest of seconds, I thought his resolution faltered. A shadow crawled over his face, but then vanished.

"My galley can carry no more than a hundred men," he said briskly, "but that will have to do. We sail for Carthage. Now."

He turned on his heel and strode to the door. I and my fellow guardsman exchanged panicked glances and hurried after him down the corridor outside.

"Sir," I cried, struggling to keep pace with his long legs, "forgive my presumption, but how can you hope to retake North Africa with just a hundred men?"

Belisarius didn't even break step. "No questions, Coel," he snapped, "my forebears never brooked questions from their subordinates. I should have you flogged. My God, would the likes of Agrippa or Agricola have put up with junior officers bleating at them? Roman discipline is much decayed."

In this mood, it was impossible to tell if he was joking. "Summon my personal guard," he added, "I will take a hundred of the best with me. Once we reach Carthage, I will call upon the garrison to join me. I left two thousand men to defend the city. More than enough."

A host of objections flew to my lips, and stayed there. I knew the general was fond of me, and also knew that he would have the skin flayed off my back if I irked him any further. Leaving him to bellow for his armour, I ran down to the barracks to rouse his guard.

We hurriedly assembled on the drill-yard outside the palace. Belisarius soon appeared, buckling on his breastplate and trailed by a group of officers, including Photius. The godlike young man looked immaculate in a gleaming silver breastplate and plumed helm, as though he had been waiting in his armour for the order to march.

His personal guard were formed into an old-fashioned maniple or cohort of five hundred men, divided into six centuries of eighty men each. They were the cream of his Veterans and bucelarii, or men like me who had performed well enough in past campaigns to be admitted to their ranks. Above all, we were men Belisarius felt he could trust on the battlefield and off it.

"First Century, with me," he shouted as our men tumbled into line, "the rest, dismissed."

I was technically appointed to the Third Century, but there was no question of me staying behind.

The eighty men of the First followed the general as he hurried down to the docks. There were a few Egyptian sailors lounging near the jetty where Belisarius' ship was moored. He pressed these unfortunates into service, roaring at them to get aboard and make ready to sail, if they valued their lives. Abandoning their games of dice, the Egyptians scrambled aboard the galley and started hauling on ropes.

We followed, pounding in double file up the gangplank. It felt as though I had barely drawn breath since Belisarius threatened to have me flogged. The wind was set fair, and my stomach gave a lurch as the mainsail billowed and the steersman turned the ship's prow south.

Over a hundred miles of open sea lay between Syracuse and Carthage. Our ship sped through the sparkling blue waters like a dolphin, propelled by Heaven-sent winds and the fierce will of Belisarius. He stood at the prow, jaw clenched, eyes fixed on the western horizon.

Meanwhile I clung to the side and emptied my breakfast into the sea. I hated myself for showing such weakness, especially in front of my comrades, even though they tactfully looked away.

"God preserve my strength," I muttered between dry heaves, touching the hilt of Caledfwlch for luck. I would need all of my grandsire's warlike skill and resolve when we reached Carthage.

We started early in the morning, and arrived within sight of the Tunisian coast just before dusk. The scattered lights of Carthage lit up the dark mass of the coastline, like thousands of yellow stars gleaming in the night sky.

Belisarius called me over to his side. "There," he said, pointing to the south of the city, "the rebel host."

I clung to a rope and squinted at a smaller gathering of lights, several miles distant of the city. If Belisarius was right, the rebels had quit Carthage and set up camp on the desolate plains outside.

"Perhaps our soldiers in the garrison found their courage, and forced them out," I said.

"We shall soon find out," he replied, "I mean to sail into the harbour and announce my presence. If we are greeted with rocks and curses, then at least we shall know who holds the city."

Our ship ghosted into the bay of Carthage. No horns or trumpets greeted our arrival, but there was no hail of missiles either. When the ship reached the chain that acted as a boom,

Belisarius ordered the imperial flag to be hoisted on the mainmast, and his trumpeter to announce our arrival with several loud blasts.

Lights flared along the sea-walls that defended the harbour to north and south. I stood in the front rank of guards behind Belisarius on the foredeck, wincing as my bowels dissolved in sickness and fear. At any moment I expected the bombardment to start, and our ship to be smashed to pieces.

Instead a small boat put out from the harbour and rowed slowly towards us. A man stood up in the belly of the boat and held a lantern aloft. The light illuminated his face, showing a youthful, bearded visage, his cheeks scarred with tattoos I recognized from my time among the Heruli.

"Who are you?" he called out in a thick Germanic accent.

"General Flavius Belisarius!" replied Belisarius in his best parade-ground bark, "and you will salute a superior officer!"

The soldier's face lit up in a grin. "General!" he cried, saluting, "thank God! We had hoped for your coming. Where is the rest of your fleet, sir?"

Belisarius threw up his hands in exasperation. "Am I a general or a schoolmaster? Every man thinks he can ask questions of me. Turn your boat around, soldier. Inform your comrades that Belisarius is here, and expects every man in the garrison to be armed and ready to ride out at dawn."

"It could be a trap," warned Bessas as the boat rowed back to shore, "how do we know the garrison is not in league with the rebels?"

"We don't," said Belisarius, "but what would you have me do? Sail around in circles until our enemies die of old age? We must act, or withdraw."

"Coel, with me," he added, nodding at me, "if you see anyone suspicious, wave your magic sword at them until they disappear."

I ignored the sarcasm and clambered down the ladder into the launch behind him. There were six boats, each large enough to carry fifteen men. Belisarius stood in the prow, his fur-trimmed red cloak thrown back to display his golden helm and ornate breastplate. He had donned ceremonial armour to dispel any doubts regarding his identity.

Like Bessas, I feared that we were heading into a trap. I crouched well behind my shield, peering over the rim to look for any archers concealed among the line of soldiers waiting for us on the docks. As we drew near they clicked their heels together and held out their right arms in a military salute.

I sagged with relief. "Welcome, General Belisarius," called out one of their officers, cupping his hands round his mouth, "we are yours to command."

6.

Belisarius wasted no time. All through the night he worked to ready the garrison to sally out at dawn. He was consumed with nervous energy, and needed no sleep, but allowed me and the rest of his guards to snatch a few hours of rest in the barracks outside the governor's residence.

The garrison was made up of foederati troops, most of them Herulii. When I woke, I sought out one of their officers and enquired what had passed since Solomon fled Carthage. He told me that after sacking the city, the rebels had marched out to meet their allies on the plains of Bulla, where two years previously I witnessed the Vandal host muster before the Battle of Tricamarum.

"As soon as they were gone, we ventured out and closed the gates," said the officer, "then we raised the imperial flag on the battlements, to show that Carthage was Roman once more."

I looked at him with contempt. "But you did nothing to protect our citizens when the rebels were running amok in the streets," I said, "and only found your courage behind strong gates and high walls. For shame."

He reddened, and flung up his hand. The Heruli, like all Germanic peoples, are fiercely proud, and quick to fall to blows.

I waited for the blow to fall. "Strike me," I said calmly, "and let it be a quarrel between us. I am happy to meet you, blade to blade, on private ground of your own choosing."

There was no-one else within earshot, otherwise he would have had no option but to accept the challenge. As it was, he confined himself to spitting at my feet, and then stalked away. Another enemy to add to the list, I thought wryly as I wiped my boot with the back of my gauntlet.

We had left our horses behind in Syracuse, but Belisarius found mounts for us in the stables of the governor's residence.

He mustered his little army on the barren ground south of the city, and harangued us just as the red orb of the morning sun rose over the hills to the east.

"Soldiers," he cried, riding back and forth across our front rank on his bay, "our enemies are cowards, and have fled inland rather than face us like men. My scouts inform me that they have forged an alliance with the degenerate Moors, and wait for us outside the city of Membresa, some fifty miles west of here. They outnumber us four to one, and have made a private soldier named Stoza their chief. He is a Roman, like us, but has broken his fealty to God and Emperor. Are we dismayed?"

Absolutely, I thought, but along with the rest of The First Century I drew my sword and held it aloft.

"Never!" we shouted. Our voices echoed across the dusty plain, and were taken up by the garrison troops formed up behind us and on the flanks. They were all light cavalry, armed with spears and large round shields. Despite their craven behaviour during the riots, Belisarius had chosen to put his faith in them. He had no choice, since there were no other troops available: all of the neighbouring Roman garrisons had thrown in their lot with the rebels.

Belisarius led us on towards Membresa, which lay beside the banks of the River Bagrades. I had never thought to set foot on African soil again, and as we rode my mind conjured up images of what I had seen and suffered in this strange land: the mad King of the Vandals, Gelimer, cackling like a crazed old woman as he raised Caledfwlch and swore to wipe the Roman army off the face of the earth; the humiliating rout of our vanguard at Ad Decimum; the blood-soaked sands of Tricamarum, where Belisarius exterminated the last Vandal host; the hell of my captivity on Mount Papua; the weeping boils that encrusted Gelimer's face and finally broke his will to resist. No, I had little reason to remember Africa with any fondness, and was anxious to quit the country again as soon as possible.

Belisarius knew that speed and surprise were essential to our slender chances of victory. Though we lacked remounts, he kept us at a furious pace, and our army arrived within sight of Membresa shortly after noon.

Membresa was a sprawling city, but undefended by walls, so the rebel host had taken up a strong position on a nearby hill. They were some eight thousand strong, a rag-bag of Arian heretics, Roman mutineers and Moors. Their commander, Stoza, knew his business, and had fortified his position with ditches and entrenchments.

Belisarius took one look at the rebel defences and shook his head.

"It won't do," I heard him say to Bessas, and he was right. A frontal assault against the rebels would be suicide, so he ordered the army to pitch camp near the banks of the river.

All through that long, hot spring day the rival hosts stood and stared at each other. Belisarius had placed his camp between Stoza's men and the city, cutting off their line of supply. His hope was that the rebels would soon run short of rations, and would have to give battle or starve.

Our own rations were limited, since we had left Carthage in haste. Belisarius solved that problem by leading three hundred of his cavalry into Membresa and forcibly taking food from the citizens. He promised to pay when the rebels were defeated and North Africa once again a Roman province, which must have been scant comfort to those he stole from.

Still the rebels would not move. Night came on, and I did my shift on watch, huddled up in my cloak and field blanket as I watched the fires on the hill. If Stoza had been a bold man, he might have tried a night assault. Belisarius was not to be taken unawares, and had half his men stand to arms while the others slept. At one hour past midnight, those who slept were shaken awake and placed on guard, while their comrades sank gratefully to rest.

I was booted awake the following morning by a grinning captain. His name was John Troglita. Like Bessas, he was another Thracian of mixed blood, and a veteran of the recent wars in Africa and Mesopotamia. He would go on to achieve general rank, but I chiefly remember him for possessing the ugliest face I have ever seen, something like a cross between a debauched wolf and a plague victim.

"Up, Briton," he snarled, jerking his thumb in the direction of the hill, "those bastards have finally decided to advance."

I rose, bucking on my sword-belt and straining to see the enemy. A strong wind had blown up during the night, whipping dust and sand across the plain.

"Damn it," I muttered, blinking and holding my arm before my face. The wind showed no signs of dying down, and an eerie howl rolled across the desert landscape, like a horde of distant wolves moaning their death-songs.

I glimpsed a multitude of spears and banners moving down from the hill. The rebels marched in poor order, especially the Moorish cavalry and camel-riders on the flanks, who had little notion of military discipline. Our Roman mutineers were easy to spot. Their infantry marched in column in the centre, with auxiliary cavalry guarding their flanks and rear.

Anger coursed through me as I watched them advance. The mutineers were still flying Roman standards, as though they were the loyalists and we the rebels.

The screech of bucinae called me to my duty. I scrambled aboard my horse and steered her towards the great imperial standard, where Belisarius was forming up his guards. He was already mounted and armed, and shading his eyes to observe the movements of the enemy across the dust-whipped plain. Photius was at his side.

Our garrison troops were a shade slower to form into line of battle, though Bessas and Troglita and other officers rode among them, screaming and striking at the laggards with iron-tipped truncheons. I galloped past the chaos and took my place in the front rank behind Belisarius.

My heart shivered at the sight of the grim mass of steel and flesh tramping towards us. The enemy numbered some eight to ten thousand, and my only solace was that Belisarius had faced worse odds before and triumphed.

I expected the rebels to march straight on and roll over our pathetic array, but instead their forward squadrons stumbled to a halt. A smile spread across my face as I watched their officers galloping to and fro, shouting and gesticulating at each other. Seeds of confusion were sown in the rebel ranks as their infantry shuffled this way and that, colliding with their comrades. War-drums and bucinae sounded a stream of conflicting orders.

Stoza was attempting to arrange his army into one long column, so their centre could engage us while the wings wrapped around our flank and rear. It wasn't a complex maneuver, but at least half his force was made up of ill-trained levies and skirmishers.

The effort proved disastrous. With the exception of the Roman troops, Stoza's entire forward line collapsed into a mob of baffled and angry men. Belisarius saw the opportunity and raised his spatha as the signal to charge.

I had taken part in many cavalry exercises outside the walls of Constantinople, learning to steer a horse with my knees while handling sword and shield, javelin and bow. I fought as part of a cavalry squadron at Ad Decimum, and witnessed the shattering assault of the bucelarii at Tricamarum, but Membresa was the first time I rode in a cavalry charge.

My sluggish blood quickens as I recall the excitement and urgency, the bunch and flow of my horse's muscles under me as I spurred her into a full-hearted gallop. The shriek of the bucinae, the roar of the men around me, the dust kicked up by hundreds of hoofs, the howl of the gale sweeping across the plain.

As we thundered into a gallop the rebel line vanished, concealed behind billowing clouds of dust and sand.

Instinct and training took over. Belisarius had drilled his guards in the use of the kontos, a slender four-metre long lance, wielded in both hands for greater thrust. The heavier shields carried by our garrison troops were a needless encumbrance to men carrying such a weapon, so instead we wore small round shields strapped to our left forearms.

I held my kontos at a low angle across my horse's neck. In this position it would outreach the weapons of the rebel infantry, and hopefully skewer any man foolish enough to hold his ground against me. Some of my comrades held their lances high, to strike and stab downwards at the enemy.

We charged blindly through the storm. The gold and silver figures of Belisarius and Photius disappeared, swallowed up inside a wall of dust. We roared in fury and drove our horses to the limit, determined not to lose sight of our beloved general for long.

The muffled yell of a trumpet sounded away to my right. Horsemen exploded into view, armed with javelins and oval shields. Stoza had thrown in his mutineer cavalry to meet our charge.

For the first time I found myself facing Romans in battle. I had no time to dwell on the irony of that, but switched my grip on the kontos, lifting it high as a horseman galloped straight at me. He hurled his javelin, but it was a poor throw. The slender dart bounced harmlessly off the boss of my shield and span away.

The impetus of his charge drove him onto my lance. I stabbed at his head, and the wickedly sharp steel tip took him in the throat and thrust out the back of his neck. I was trained for this, and gave the kontos a sharp twist, withdrawing the tip even as the mutineer fell from his saddle, blood pumping from the neat hole in his neck.

Now all our ranks were broken up, the fight dissolved into dozens of individual combats. Dust flew into my eyes. A shape hurled itself at me, screaming like a devil, and I felt something hammer against my ribs. The pain made me cry out and double over. A javelin had hit me in the side, but my fine scale armour had preserved me from worse than bruises.

My kontos was virtually useless in this sort of close fighting. I hurled it away and ripped out Caledfwlch, feeling my courage return as my fingers closed around the worn ivory grip.

Most of my comrades fought with spathas, long swords with a heavy chopping edge. Caledfwlch was a gladius, a much shorter and rather antiquated weapon, intended for stabbing rather than hacking with the edge. Many of the guards thought me vain for persisting with such a relic, but I found the shorter blade gave me an advantage at close quarters.

I wiped my eyes with the back of my hand, just as the shrieking wind tore away the veil of dust and sand before us. At last I could see the rebel infantry, or what was left of it. Belisarius' wild storm-charge had smashed great holes in their ranks, sweeping away squadrons and littering the ground with broken and mutilated bodies.

Many of the ill-armed levies had fled the field, but a few stubborn mutineers and Vandals remained, formed up in isolated groups around their standards. Our cavalry swirled around them, casting spears and javelins in their faces.

Belisarius' guards were trained to use the short bow while mounted, and thumbed arrows into the helpless rebels. They would die where they stood, these men, or face the agony of crucifixion as a just punishment for those who betrayed the Roman state.

I turned my horse away, thinking to take a breath of air and some water from my pottle. Now the brief battle was all but won, there was no need to take undue risks. Our men would whittle away at the rebels until their ragged shield-walls broke and we could charge in for the final slaughter.

My horse carried me clear of the stench and din of battle, until I found a relatively quiet spot. The wind was still churning up sand-devils and blowing clouds of dust across the plain, so I felt strangely alone, shielded from the slaughter happening not more than thirty feet away.

I had forgotten about Photius. He might have killed me then, but was unable to restrain himself from letting out a cry as he raced in to cut me down from behind.

My water pottle was halfway to my lips when I heard the cry. I dropped it and hurled myself out of the saddle. His spatha sliced through thin air as I crashed onto my side, painfully jarring my recently healed arm.

"Pig!" I heard Photius snarl. He galloped past and wrenched his horse around for another tilt at me. I glimpsed the young man's face under his helmet, his handsome features contorted almost beyond recognition with berserk fury.

Some instinct made me glance to my left. Another horseman was coming at me, one of my comrades from the First, his kontos lowered at my breast.

The ground shook under my feet as he charged. Somehow my nerve held. Instead of panicking I held my ground and watched that gleaming lance-tip streak towards me. At the very last second I dived to my left.

Death missed me by inches. I hit the ground hard, staggered to my feet, spitting dirt, and turned to face where I imagined Photius was.

Too late. He was on me like an avenging angel, spatha raised to strike. I had no time to lift my little shield or ward off his blow with Caledfwlch.

His blade crashed against the side of my helmet. Searing pain filled my skull. I tasted blood in my mouth. The world vanished, replaced by darkness and flashing lights.

Then there was nothing.

7.

I must have lain unconscious for several hours. When I woke, night was slanting across the battlefield, and the thumping pain in my head was as nothing to the stench of death in my nostrils.

Happily, Photius was not half the swordsman he thought he was. His blow had sheared the side-flap from my helmet, and scored a nasty gash on my head, but failed to split the bone. It was enough to knock me out cold, and fool him into leaving me for dead, but I suffered no other damage save a headache and loss of blood.

I peeled off the crumpled shell of my helmet and struggled into a kneeling position, groaning and carefully exploring the wound on my head. The bleeding had stopped, and the right side of my skull was covered in a layer of half-dried, congealed gore.

There was no sign of our army. The freak storm had died down, and I was able to see the hundreds of bodies, men and horses, that carpeted the plain. Most of them were rebels. Belisarius had smashed Stoza's host and moved on, either pursuing them into the deep desert or withdrawing to Carthage. I briefly felt bitter that he had left me behind, but that was naive: victory came first, and Belisarius could not afford to be sentimental.

The feeble groans of the dying echoed across the field as I got to my feet. My head swam, and I swayed dangerously, like a new-born calf attempting to stand.

My hand instinctively went to my hip, searching for the reassuring touch of ivory. The scabbard was empty. Gulping in panic, I glanced down and spotted the sword lying near where I had fallen. It seemed Photius was ignorant of the legend of Caesar's sword, and had not thought to take it.

Other voices reached my ears as I bent to pick up Caledfwlch. The moans of dying men were mingled with the shrill yelps of desert hyenas, prowling among the bodies and fighting each other for strips of carrion. Some of the vile beasts tore at the bodies of men that yet lived. I saw a few vultures flapping about, their great leathery wings lending them the appearance of witches.

Their human counterparts were at work. Some of the braver or more desperate citizens of Membresa had ventured out of the city, carrying knives and cudgels. Now the fighting was over, it was time to plunder the dead as some recompense for being robbed by Belisarius.

I had witnessed the aftermath of battles before, but never from a position of danger. If I didn't get off the field and find somewhere to hide until dawn, I would end up with a slashed throat, and Caledfwlch would fall into peasant hands.

My wound made me sluggish. I had scarcely begun to limp away when a high-pitched, nasally voice cried out somewhere behind me:

"There is one of them! Bring him down!"

I broke into a staggering run. More voices piped up, like a flock of excited crows descending on a kill.

A number of thin, wiry figures in loose grey robes suddenly appeared before me, as though they had sprouted out of the ground. They were peasants, their seamed, leathery faces twisted into bestial snarls, gnarled hands gripping sickles and pitchforks and other makeshift weapons.

I fell into a guard position, holding Caledwlch ready to stab at any that came too near. The peasants were not dissuaded, and slowly closed in around me.

"This one has some fire left in him," one grunted, "bring him down with your spear, Sama."

The vinegar-faced brute named Sama drew back his arm and left fly. Fortunately, he was a handless buffoon, and the sharpened stick that he called a spear flew harmlessly over my head.

I swallowed and moistened my dry lips, cudgeling my brain for something to say. "I am a Roman officer," I croaked, unable to think of anything better, "if you harm me, Rome will have her vengeance. Let me go, and you shall be rewarded."

Months later, when I repeated this little speech to Procopius, he laughed until the tears flowed down his cheeks.

"Poor Coel," he chuckled, dabbing at his eyes, "your continued survival is proof that God has a certain dry wit."

He was right, damn him. I should have spared my breath. Staying strong and silent might have made the peasants hesitate, but now they knew I was desperate. And scared.

"Take him!" cried one who seemed to be their leader, a round-shouldered man with a greasy tangle of beard poking from under the scarf that hid the lower part of his face. He had a certain authority, and his robe and fringed mantle were made of finer stuff than the coarse wool of his fellows.

He was also no fool, and hung back while the others rushed me all at once. There were seven of them, too many to repel even I had been fit.

I had no option but to try. A man wielding a pitchfork came screaming at me, jabbing the prongs at my face. I batted the clumsy weapon away and sheared the skin off his knuckles, making him drop the fork and howl in agony.

A flat-headed wooden club cracked against my shoulder. Once again my armour saved me. I swung around to stab at the clubman, and someone grabbed my hair from behind. That was futile, since it was shorn to a smear of stubble, Roman military style. I jerked my head backwards and connected sharply with a jaw.

My satisfaction at the muffled curse that followed was short-lived. Something struck me in the stomach, expelling all the breath from my lungs. Fingers closed around my wrist, and I was unable to lift Caledfwlch.

"Slash the Roman thief's throat!" someone yelled. I felt cold steel pressed against my neck.

"No, no," cried their chief, "let him live for now. Spare him for the games."

The men holding me grumbled, and the one with the knife had murder in his eyes, but the round-shouldered man was clearly in command. From his superior dress and manner I judged him to be some elder or dignitary from the city.

Despite his authority, he still had to wheedle a little. "Think, brothers," he said in a voice dripping with insinuation, "how we might put this fine Roman officer to the test. Will he last longer than the usual thieves and cut-purses? The Romans make their soldiers tough, so they say. They will not beg for mercy, nor reveal any secrets under torture. Let us challenge that proud boast."

His words made me quail, but I tried to maintain a stoic front while the peasants laughed and nudged each other. It seemed that the prospect of breaking my body with various unspeakable tortures held more appeal than simply killing me on the spot, quick and clean.

"Give me his sword," ordered their chief. I stifled a cry as Caledfwlch was torn from my grip and handed reverently to him, like an offering to a priest.

"Pretty," the devil murmured, his deep-set eyes squinting at the blade as he inspected it, "a fine toy for my children to play with."

I worked up some pointless defiance. "If you have managed to breed," I rasped, "then there is hope for every ape in Africa."

"I shall enjoy you," he said, tucking Caledfwlch into the sash around his waist, "I shall enjoy you very much indeed."

They took me into the city, a sprawling and ramshackle place, designed in no particular order or pattern that I could see. As I have said, it had no walls, or drains either judging from the stink. The people were mostly white-skinned Africans mixed with a few Moors. They spat and jeered at me as I was pushed through the streets.

"Look at the great Roman warrior!" they mocked, "see the power of Caesar, and tremble! Shall we bow down before you, soldier, and offer tribute?"

Roman rule was not popular in North Africa, largely thanks to Justinian's grinding taxes. Belisarius had all but crushed the revolt, and the people of Membresa would soon become part of the Empire again, so this was their last chance to express their resentment of imperial rule.

I was the focus of that resentment. Had it not been for the chieftain, who held back the mob with an extraordinary flow of eloquence – and if that failed, a heavy stick – I would have been torn to pieces long before we reached the prisons.

These were a block of crude single-storey cells built against the eastern wall of the largest residence in the city, a domed and porticoed house that I assumed to be the governor's dwelling. They were all full, but a space was made for me by the simple expedient of clearing out all the inmates from one cell and cramming them into the others.

"Courage," one of the other prisoners gasped as he was dragged past me, "the general will save us."

He was dirty and blooded, but with a start I recognized him as Constantine, one of Belisarius' captains. Another casualty from the battle, left for dead on the field and taken prisoner.

I was shoved into a dark, foul-smelling chamber with a few wisps of dirty straw scattered on the earthen floor. The iron gate swung shut behind me.

"Rest there, Roman," cackled the jailer, a grey-toothed savage with a cast in one eye, "rest there until we decide to play with you."

A few more insults were thrown at me, along with a final burst of spittle, and then they left me alone to brood.

At least, I reflected as I slumped to the floor and rested my back against the slimy wall, I had been in worse places. The dungeons of the Praetorium in Constantinople were no less uncomfortable. Nor was the griddle that Theodora would have roasted me alive on, had I not been saved by Narses.

There was little chance of a rescue here, in this remote flyblown part of Africa. Men always cling to hope, and I dared to dream that Belisarius would send a troop of cavalry in search of me. If not for my sake alone, then to retrieve Caledfwlch. Julius Caesar's sword could not be allowed to fall into enemy hands.

Darkness fell across the city. There was no light in my dingy prison, but the barred door faced out onto the torch-lit market square, which was slowly filling up with people. A few of them hurled curses at me, but most of their attention was fixed on a raised platform or dais being constructed in the middle of the square.

The night was cold, but an extra chill flowered in the pit of my stomach as I watched the dais take shape. Another team of workmen brought a wagon into the square, pulled by a team of ponies, and lifted three long iron stakes off the back. The gathering crowd cheered as the stakes were hoisted onto the dais and fixed horizontally into three stone bases. They were about eight feet tall, and thrust into the air like lances, razor-sharp at one end.

My brow furrowed as I watched a type of gallows erected next to the row of stakes. Then I realised it was a crude winch, considerably higher than the stakes, with a rope thrown over the cross-bar.

More wagons arrived, carrying great stone jars containing some form of strong drink. These were passed among the crowd. People quickly became drunk and quarrelsome, and fights started to break out. No-one bothered to quell them. I ignored the violence and watched the men on the dais. They carried pots full of oil or grease, and were rubbing the stuff on the stakes.

My skin crawled. I am blessed or cursed with a prodigious imagination, and my mind conjured up depraved images of the torments that would soon be inflicted on my shrinking carcass. I had heard rumours of the foul punishments inflicted on criminals in the more remote provinces, and never imagined that I might be the subject of them.

"Belisarius will come," I muttered to myself, over and over, "Belisarius will come…"

Somewhere a drum started to beat, and the more excitable or drunken spirits in the crowd set up a great howling, like the jackals in the desert.

A group of watchmen in ill-fitting leather tunics and helmets marched over to the prison houses. My heart lurched as I thought they would come to mine first. Shamefully, I prayed otherwise, and God heard my prayer. The watchmen chose one of the cells at the end of the row and dragged out the unfortunates held inside.

Their wrists were bound behind their backs, and they were kicked and whipped towards the dais. I thought the crowd would set upon them, but instead a lane opened for the prisoners to pass through.

One of them was Constantine. He looked around, wild-eyed, until he spotted me.

"The general will come!" he shouted, until a laughing watchman clapped a hand over his mouth.

"He will not," I mouthed silently, leaning against the bars of my cell door.

There were five prisoners. Three of them, including the Heruli, were hauled up the wooden steps onto the dais. The other two were held below to wait their turn.

The games, as the African chieftain termed them, were not very sophisticated. My gorge rose as I realised what was going to happen.

By now the noise in the square was unbearable. Wild, blood-curdling shrieks filled the air. The people wanted their entertainment.

They soon got it. The three men on the dais lost the last shreds of their dignity as their clothes were cut away, and their ankles bound as well as their wrists. Helpless, the first of them was pulled over to the winch, and one end of the rope tied about his neck.

My mind refused to believe what I was about to witness. The cruelties and debaucheries of the imperial court in Constantinople were nothing compared to this. Even Theodora would baulk at it.

As a final indignity, and an aid to the obscenity about to follow, the suffering man's fundament was slit open with a knife, and some kind of paste slapped onto the wound. As he screamed and wept for mercy, for Jesus, for his mother, six strong men seized hold of the other end of the rope and hauled him into the air.

They might have held him there, suspended by his neck, until he was strangled, but that was not the aim. The cross-bar of the winch overhung all three of the iron stakes, and he was lowered down onto the first.

I screwed my eyes shut and held onto the bars for support as his scream split the night sky. The agony that poor wretch suffered was unimaginable, and yet it would soon be my turn.

It has been many years since I gave up earthly vanities. God and Abbot Gildas have no use for them, and so I have no hesitation in recording that I wept. Wept like a frightened child, in stark terror for the unspeakable death that I was doomed to suffer. What mirthless, random Fate had brought me to this pass, after so many vicissitudes of fortune? Could I, the last prince of the old royal blood of Coel Hen, really be destined to die such a vile and humiliating death, thousands of miles from my homeland?

The man impaled on the stake screamed and screamed, even as those devils laughed and capered in delight at his sufferings. I could not bear to watch or hear, and retreated to the furthest wall of the prison, clapping my hands over my ears.

I feared my sanity might crack under the strain. The screams redoubled as another of the poor wretches was hoisted to his doom, though at least their cries of torment were partially drowned by the excited shrieks and laughter of the crowd.

A shadow fell over me. I looked up and saw the silhouette of the round-shouldered chieftain. He was leaning against the bars of the prison door, regarding me with narrowed eyes. Two larger men stood behind him, holding torches.

"This one is next," he said, "open the door."

His words were death. I stood up, looking around in vain for some kind of weapon, anything, while the jailer fumbled with his keys. The floor was worn smooth and bare of anything save straw.

The door creaked open, whining on its rusted hinges. I dropped into a crouch. At the very least, I could spring on the chieftain and snap his neck with my bare hands – a trick the Heruli taught me – before his men dragged me off him.

I was about to leap, but hesitated as he produced Caledfwlch. "See, Roman," he taunted, holding it up before me, "I thought you might like to look upon your precious sword once more."

"Here," he added, and suddenly his voice sounded quite different, "take a closer look."

To my astonishment, he tossed Caledwlch at my feet. Then he straightened from his stooped, round-shouldered stance, tore away the scarf and wisp of false beard from his face, and there stood no sneering African chieftain at all, but Procopius.

"Close your mouth, Coel," he snapped, "and pick up the sword. We have no time to waste on explanations."

I bit back my questions and snatched up Caledfwlch. Belisarius claimed he felt nothing when he handled the blade, but then he had no hereditary right to it. I felt renewed as soon as my hand closed around the hilt.

Procopius' guards stepped into the cell. They shrugged back their hoods, and I could have laughed with delight as I recognized the brutish faces of the Huns who had guarded me during the voyage to Sicily. One of them grinned and ducked his oversized head at me, while his comrade seized the terrified jailer and twisted his neck, like a farmer strangling a goose.

"We have horses waiting, just outside," said Procopius, "step quickly, before those clods outside realise what is afoot."

He moved briskly to the door, beckoning at me to follow. I feared we would be spotted, but all the attention of the crowd was fixed on the two men writhing on the stakes. I averted my eyes from the grisly spectacle as we hurried down the street, but then I remembered the third man on the dais, waiting his turn for execution.

"We have to get him out," I hissed, seizing Procopius' arm and jabbing my sword at the dais, "he is a Roman, like us. We can't leave him to be butchered by these savages."

"Don't be an idiot," replied Procopius, brushing me off, but the Huns grunted in agreement. The secretary was not a soldier, and failed to understand that one didn't simply leave a comrade to his fate.

Understanding soon dawned, though, when he looked at our faces. "For God's sake," he muttered, and threw up his hands, "very well. But don't expect any peace in the afterlife if all goes awry."

There were four horses tethered to a rail outside a wine-shop at the end of the street. Mine was a pure white desert pony, a high-spirited beast, and must have cost Procopius a fair amount of silver. I climbed aboard her, feeling like a soldier again instead of the sniveling, broken wreck I had been just moments before.

Now some of the more alert souls in the square had noticed that one of the cells was empty, and the inmate flown. A few rushed down the street, yelling indignantly and waving torches.

They froze at the sight of us. I heeled my pony into life and urged her towards them, snarling in anticipation of drawing blood. I wanted to pay these barbarians back for the fright they had given me.

Procopius and the Huns galloped close behind me. The citizens scattered out of our path and vanished down a side-alley. Then we were into the square. Scores of pale faces turned to greet us. I bellowed a war-cry, ducked low over my pony's neck and thrust Caledfwlch at the nearest body.

The blade ripped through muscle and flesh with satisfying ease, drenching my sword-hand in blood up to the wrist. My victim jerked as I tore Caledfwlch free, and dropped to the ground like a doll with its strings cut.

Most of the citizens had panicked and were fleeing in all directions. The bravest – or drunkest – showed some fight, and one swung a hatchet at my pony's head. I drew back savagely on the reins, snapping her head back, and one of the Huns flung a spear through the man's body.

Now the dais rose before me. Constantine stood on the edge, stripped naked and looking almost comical as he shuffled feverishly from side to side, trying to loosen the bonds on his ankles.

His bulging eyes were fixed on me. I couldn't shout at him to jump – his weight would have flattened my pony – so I slid from the saddle and ran up the steps to the platform.

I averted my eyes from the poor wretches impaled on the stakes, and ran to my comrade. He trembled as I sawed at the bindings on his wrists and ankles.

"Hurry, brother," he cried, "before the barbarians find their courage."

I glanced down at the square. One of the Huns had seized hold of my pony's bridle, to prevent her bolting, while his comrade was single-handedly holding back the mob.

He wielded two curved swords, both red with blood, and clashed them both against his armoured chest, screaming like a madman and glaring at the citizens, daring them to fight him. They cowered and declined the challenge, as any sane man would. The Huns are the fiercest warriors alive, matched only by the Sarmatians, and I often had cause to thank God they were on my side.

Procopius gestured impatiently at me. "Move!" he shouted. He had a long dagger in his hand, though I always found it difficult to imagine him wielding anything more deadly than a stylus.

The bonds parted, and Constantine gasped as the blood flowed back into his numbed limbs. There was a spear lying against the base of the winch, abandoned by the cowardly executioners when they fled. He grabbed it and performed an act of mercy, stabbing it through the hearts of the men dying by inches on the stakes.

I seized his arm and led him down the steps. "Here," cried Procopius, "my horse is big enough to carry two."

He helped Constantine to mount, while I returned to my own horse, nodding in thanks to the Hun who held his bridle.

Seeing us on the verge of escape, the mob surged forward. The Hun who stood in their way snarled and made his horse rear onto her haunches. Her flailing hoofs made them hesitate, but then a youth ran forward and thrust his torch at the horse's face. She screamed and twisted away from the flame, spilling her rider and crashing onto her flank.

The Hun was a big man, but lithe as an acrobat, and rolled to his feet with extraordinary grace. Three men attacked him at once, baying like dogs. His swords moved in a blur, and one of the men toppled to the ground, blood pumping from the stump of his neck. His neatly severed head bounced and rolled away. The Hun disemboweled the second man, slashed the throat of the third, and was then overwhelmed by a sea of enraged bodies.

"Come away," said Procopius, "he cannot be saved."

The remaining Hun was of a different opinion. Instead of obeying his master, he spurred his horse into the howling mob as they hacked and stabbed at his comrade.

My courage was exhausted, and I had no intention of joining the Huns in death. I caught one last glimpse of them standing back-to-back, singing their death-songs as they fought with desperate fury.

I raised Caledfwlch in salute to their heroism, and wheeled my pony to follow Procopius out of the city.

8.

No pursuit followed us during the fifty-mile dash from Membresa to Carthage. Either the people of the city lacked horsemen, or their spirit had been knocked out of them by the bloody last stand of the Huns.

This was fortunate, for Procopius' horse could not carry two men at the gallop over a long distance. For most of the way we rode at an easy canter. To me our progress was nightmarishly slow, and I cast anxious glances over my shoulder, expecting to see the dark shapes of riders on the horizon.

We rode through the night, and the morning sun was already high in the sky by the time we arrived within sight of Carthage. I was drooping with fatigue, and could scarcely keep my eyes open to take in the blessed sight of the city's ancient walls.

Constantine was in an even more pitiful state. Snatched from the jaws of a hideous death, obliged to ride naked over fifty miles of rough ground, he was overcome as we rode through the city gates, and slid quietly from the saddle.

The guards on the gate recognized him, and helped us to scrape the fallen man off the cobbles and carefully lift him onto a stretcher fetched from the guardroom. Their captain was full of tender concern for a fellow soldier, and went puce when I told him what had passed at Membresa.

"Those filthy, dung-ball savages," he exclaimed, shaking his fist in the vague direction of the city, "if I was Belisarius, I would lead the garrison out in force again and crucify every living thing in Membresa, down to the last babe in arms."

"Is the general still in Carthage?" asked Procopius.

"No. He sailed yesterday for Sicily. Word reached here of some mutiny in the garrison at Syracuse. He left Hildiger and Theodore in charge until Solomon returns."

Hildiger and Theodore were two of Belisarius' subordinates. The general must have withdrawn immediately to Carthage after his victory at Membresa, which meant the rebellion in North Africa was not quite extinguished.

"It seems Belisarius is doomed to spend his days rushing from one crisis to another, stamping out fires wherever they spring up," said Procopius as our comrade was carried to the palace, "I had hoped to find him here."

I was so tired I could barely stand, but full of questions. He forestalled them by placing a finger to my lips.

"Peace," he said with a rare gleam of kindness, "you look ready to collapse, and I prefer not to trouble the captain for another stretcher. Go to the barracks and sleep. I will tell you all on the voyage back to Sicily."

There was no question of returning to Sicily. We were both sworn to serve Belisarius, and Rome, and had no further purpose in Africa. I was only too glad to leave that benighted continent behind me for the second time.

After I had slept a full day, washed, eaten and felt something like a man again, I was summoned by Procopius to his private quarters on the upper floors of the palace. Naturally, his quarters were of the best, and had a balcony overlooking the harbour and the Gulf of Tunis. A slave admitted me, and I found Procopius drinking wine in the company of Constantine.

I returned Constantine's bow, noting how different he seemed, washed and rested and back in uniform. Something of the visceral terror of Membresa remained in the depths of his blue eyes. I, who had suffered my share of near scrapes with death, knew that the memory of those iron stakes would never leave his nightmares.

The formalities done, he seized me in a warm embrace. "My saviour," he cried, "I shall forever be in your debt, for as long as breath lasts in this body."

I thought he might start weeping on my neck, and stared helplessly at a grinning Procopius. Thankfully Constantine desisted.

"Procopius has told me your name, and your quality," he said, stepping back and recovering some of his military poise, "you are a prince of the old blood of Albion. I am honoured to know you, Coel ap Amhar ap Arthur. I bear the name of one of your royal ancestors. Constantine the Great is said to have had a British mother, herself the daughter of Coel Hen."

"The honour is all mine, Constantine," I replied with a wary smile, "and it is always good to make new friends. You must not consider yourself in debt to me, though. Debts make men resentful."

"Not this man," he said, thumping his fist against his chest, "but for you, I would be rotting in the desert sun. Do not talk of resentment. Such ignoble sentiments do not exist between men of honour like us."

I wasn't convinced that I was a man of honour, particularly, but it seemed a shame to disappoint him. I let the matter drop and accepted a cup of wine from Procopius.

"All is arranged," he said, "I have hired a vessel to take us to Syracuse this evening."

I groaned at the prospect of another trial by sea. "At least it is a short voyage. What news of the mutiny in Syracuse?"

Procopius gestured vaguely. "Nothing yet. Some revolt over pay, I understand. Belisarius will whip the curs to heel. God help the Roman state if he falls overboard in the Gulf of Tunis, or trips on landing and breaks his neck. The Empire could not survive the death of Belisarius."

"Oh, come," I replied, "he is a good soldier, perhaps the best since Aetius, but Rome has other men to lead her armies. What of Mundus, and Bessas, and others like them?"

He swept these names aside with a sweep of his hand. "Pygmies," he said dismissively, "competent enough, I grant you, but base of soul. Hirelings and mercenaries. Only Belisarius has something of the spark in him that animated the Romans of old. It is difficult to describe."

"A greatness of spirit," said Constantine, who had listened to our exchange with interest, "he fights, not for himself, but for the greater glory of the Empire. Money and fame and personal glory are of little importance to him."

I disagreed with that, since during the course of his campaigns Belisarius had made himself a very wealthy man. He loved ceremony, and being the focus of attention, and had accepted all the elaborate glories heaped on him by Justinian without a qualm. Another man might have refused the rank of Consul, which had been in abeyance for centuries, as an outdated absurdity.

However, I was in no mood to argue, and something about my companions' manner made me uneasy. I detected a hint of fanaticism in Procopius' voice, and there was an intensity about Constantine that I disliked. My naturally sceptical nature prevented me from succumbing to the worship of so-called great men. I knew, all too well, the vices and failings of one of the greatest of all, my grandsire Arthur, and cannot help but smile when I hear the fables and legends in which he features as a sort of demi-god, a perfect warrior and immortal saviour of his people.

I changed the subject, and asked Procopius how he had come to rescue myself and Constantine from the stakes. As vain as he was clever, the secretary loved to speak of himself and his deeds, and preened a little before launching into the tale.

"It was well for you both that I chose to rise from my sick-bed in Syracuse," he said, "and take ship for Carthage shortly after

Belisarius left. Solomon's failure to crush the rebels was, I felt, partially my own, and I wished to make amends."

He paused to glance out of the doorway at the glistening blue seas beyond, and savour the taste of his wine. "I reached Carthage to find that Belisarius had already ridden out – none can match the speed of that man, when his blood is roused! Determined to be in at the death, I followed the trail of the army, only to meet his vanguard returning from the battle. The rebels were already defeated, and Stoza and his survivors driven into the desert. Belisarius stopped to talk with me. He was greatly distressed by your disappearance, Coel, and ordered me to search the battlefield for any sign of you."

I felt a twinge of guilt. Belisarius had not simply abandoned me after all. For him to worry over the fate of one lowly officer argued that he was indeed the great man his admirers claimed him to be.

My cynicism asserted itself. "He wanted Caledfwlch," I said, "he wanted my sword, so he could take it back to Constantinople and hide it away somewhere in a palace strongroom."

"If all Belisarius wanted was your sword," Procopius replied tartly, "then he could take it easily enough. You are but one man, Coel."

He resumed his tale. "I knew that scavengers would be prowling the battlefield. Subtlety was called for, so I assumed the guise of an African nobleman, and arrived in Membresa claiming to be an equerry from Stoza. I speak many languages, and have some skill as an actor. Stoza was not beaten, I assured the citizens, but would raise a new army in the desert and return to sweep the Romans out of North Africa. The fools warmed to my words, and after that I had little difficulty manipulating them."

He plucked a purple grape from the bunch on a silver dish on the table between us, and winked at me as he peeled it.

"You see, Coel, I have many layers," he said, popping the grape into his mouth, "my mother, God rest her, often said I was six souls packed into one body. Shrewd woman."

His complacency was laughable, but not without foundation. Shamefully, I had not yet thanked him for saving me, and did so with all due humility.

"Enough of that," he said carelessly, flapping a languid hand at me, "you are not the first I have rescued. Some men perform their duty in the battle-line with sword and shield. I do mine in other ways."

I finished my wine and left them, claiming that I was still tired and needed my rest before enduring another voyage. That was true enough, but I had had my fill of their unsettling company. Constantine kept staring at me with disturbing intensity, and I was beginning to suspect that Procopius had only rescued me for some dark purpose of his own.

If I sound suspicious and ungrateful, do not judge me too harshly. Years of living among the Romans made me so. They are a dark and artful people, jealous of their diminished power and prestige, and stop at nothing to get what they want. Even at this stage of my life, I had not yet been exposed to the worst of the Roman character.

We embarked the following morning, just as the sun was rising over the sea. Procopius had hired a small galley, light and swift, and our journey across the Gulf was mercifully quick.

The galley sailed into the harbour at Syracuse at dusk. Belisarius' banners flew from the ramparts and the towers of the palace, and all seemed peaceful inside the city as it basked in the warmth of a spring evening.

"Yes, the general's here," said an Isaurian bowman we encountered lounging outside a wine-shop on the docks, "and like to be here for some time. The invasion of Italy's off."

"Off?" squawked Procopius, "what do you mean, off?"

The Isaurian yawned and rubbed his unshaven chin. "I'm no politico," he replied, "but it seems the King of the Goths has lost his nerve. Our conquest of Sicily scared the shit out of him, and he's offered the Emperor a heap of gold and silver to leave Italy alone. If Caesar is a sensible man, he'll take the money."

"I must recommend your appointment to the imperial council," Procopius said coldly.

He was angry, more at being ignorant of current events than anything. When we reached the palace he demanded loudly to see Belisarius, and with breathtaking arrogance swept through the guards and slaves as though they weren't there.

Had Procopius been anyone else, he might have received a sword in his gut, for the men who guarded Belisarius took no chances. As it happened, his face and manner were well-known, and we were admitted to the general's private chambers.

Belisarius was poring over a heap of maps and parchment by candlelight when we were ushered in, and let out a cry at the sight of us.

"Coel – alive!" he shouted, striding across the room to seize my hand, "I hardly dared to hope. We lost too many good men at Membresa. And you, Constantine!"

He embraced us both, and gave Procopius a playful punch on the arm. "I'm not surprised to see you alive and whole," he laughed, "I believe you would find a safe passage through Hell. Where did you find my two deserters, then?"

Belisarius was in high good humour, and his secretary knew better than to spoil the mood with boasts. "I plucked them out of a stew," he replied modestly, "the details of it are rather dull and routine. What of Italy, sir?"

Belisarius threw up his hands. "What of Italy, indeed! Well, there she lies, just a few miles off the coast of Sicily, and for now her southern mainland is open to invasion. King Theodatus wastes our time with talk. He has offered Justinian all manner of concessions. The yielding of Sicily to the Empire, yearly tribute of a crown weighing three hundred pounds in gold, a promise to supply three thousand Gothic auxiliaries to help defend our borders…all this, and much more, has he offered our ambassador in Ravenna."

Myself and Constantine may as well have been shadows in the background. This was politics now, Procopius' preferred battleground, and we could do naught but listen and learn.

"What of the war in Dalmatia?" he asked pointedly. I was dismayed when Belisarius gave a heavy sigh and sagged onto the stool beside his desk.

"Defeat and disaster," he said wearily, "the news was waiting for me when I returned. Our army pushed back the Goths and stormed Salona, but then Gothic reinforcements appeared. Mundus's son, the fool, sallied out against them, and was unhorsed and killed in sight of the walls. Mundus lost his head completely, as any father might when confronted with the death of his son, and led out the remainder of the garrison in a wild charge. They were destroyed, and Mundus slain. What was left of our army fled back over the frontier into Illyria."

He grimaced, and pinched the bridge of his nose. For the first time I noticed the deep crease between his eyes, an indelible mark of worry and responsibility.

The news of our defeat in Dalmatia was shattering, but Procopius betrayed no hint of emotion. "Theodatus is now free to transfer men from Dalmatia to Italy," he said. "If we are to strike, we must strike now, sir, before the mainland fills with barbarian troops."

"I am waiting for word from the Emperor," Belisarius said firmly, "I will do nothing without his sanction. Besides which, I have just quelled a mutiny here, and Stoza is still alive and at liberty in Africa. We must do nothing rash."

That, judging from his drawn and haggard appearance, was a veiled wish for rest. Having conquered Sicily and saved North Africa, Belisarius must have feared that Justinian would now dispatch him to rescue the situation in Dalmatia. After that, what next? Would he be packed off to the eastern fringes of the Empire, to fight the Sassanids again, or sent back to Africa to hunt down Stoza and exterminate the troublesome Moors?

God had seen fit to grant Belisarius victory after victory. At some point his luck and favour would run out. Assuming, of course, that he didn't simply collapse and die of exhaustion first.

I ventured to interrupt. "Where is Photius, sir?" I asked, "did he survive the battle?"

Procopius looked at me in anger and disbelief at my lack of subtlety, but I was not minded to play his games. Ever since our escape from Membresa, I had brooded over Photius' attempt on my life, and was determined to pay him back in kind. As Constantine might have said, it was a matter of honour.

Belisarius looked surprised by the question. "Photius? Yes, he is alive. I sent him to Palermo to be with his mother. She prefers the north of the island. Why do you ask?"

Palermo. My vengeance would have to be delayed. "I saw him in the thickest of the battle," I replied with an offhand shrug, "it grieved me to think that such a promising young man might have been slain."

He smiled and patted my shoulder, pleased that I showed such concern for his beloved wife's son. "You have a generous heart," he said, "and Photius is indeed a promising youth. Headstrong, of course, but so was I at that age."

He invited us to stay for dinner, and over the meal described more of the diplomatic sparring between Ravenna and Constantinople. It seemed that Theodatus was ready to promise anything to deter the wrath of Rome. There was even some talk of him abdicating, if Justinian should wish it.

We remained idle in Syracuse for the next few weeks, waiting for orders from the Emperor. Photius did not return from Palermo, and Procopius dissuaded me from going in search of him.

"No good would come of it, even if you slew him," he said, "Belisarius would have no choice but to hang you for a murderer. Do not imagine that the death of her son would cause Antonina much grief. She is not a loving mother, and uses Photius as just another tool to achieve her ends."

I was content to wait. Photius had tried to murder me, no doubt at his mother's instigation, amid the noise and confusion of battle. I would bide my time, until the opportunity arose to serve him the same way. A blade in the dark, perhaps, when he was staggering back from a night's drinking. There were ways and means, and it was tempting to hire a band of killers to do the work for me.

These happy thoughts occupied my time, and I briefly resumed my desultory affair with the shopkeeper's daughter. There were other women, and my memory of that time is of a long, hazy summer, the last golden afterglow of youth and beauty.

Reality intruded with the onset of autumn, and the arrival of a messenger from the imperial court. Belisarius was closeted with him for several hours, along with his captains and Procopius.

After the meeting had broken up, Procopius sought me out in a taverna near the palace. He looked happy, which was ominous, for that usually meant trouble for someone.

"Best sharpen that old sword of yours, Coel," he said, drawing up an extra stool and helping himself to my wine.

"The invasion is on again?" I asked through a mouthful of bread and olives.

"It is indeed. King Theodatus's recent victories in Dalmatia have poured a little steel into the old man's wilting spine. Three days ago he declared the proposed treaty null and void, broke his vow of peace, and seized and imprisoned our ambassadors in Ravenna. Justinian is furious, and has ordered Belisarius to invade Italy and topple Theodatus from his throne."

I listened to this with mixed feelings. I was a soldier, and war was my trade, but I had grown comfortable in Sicily, and was reluctant to set out on what promised to be a hellish campaign.

"Belisarius is all energy and purpose," Procopius added, "enough men will be left behind to garrison Palermo and Syracuse, but the bulk of our forccs will concentrate at Messina."

He picked up a chunk of bread as he spoke, and tore off pieces to represent our army and the planned invasion.

"From Messina," - he picked up the largest crumb and pushed it towards me - "we will cross into Reggio via the Strait of Messina! It could not be better."

"What do you mean?" I asked, frowning at him.

"Tut! Do you not recall your Greek history? No, I see you do not. God knows what kind of stunted education you received in that damp, misty northern island you call home. The Strait of Messina is home to Scylla and Charybdis."

I must have looked blank, for he rolled his eyes at my ignorance. "Scylla and Charybdis," he explained patiently, "were noted by the Greek historian Homer as sea-monsters that guarded the crossing between Sicily and the Italian mainland. He described Scylla as a six-headed serpent, and Charybdis as a kind of giant beast that dwelled on the seabed, waiting for ships to come along so she could drag them down and devour them, vessels, crew, and all."

I had been raised to believe in the various fantastic beasts and monsters that populate British legends – pink-eared hounds, white harts, witches and giants and the monstrous razor-backed boar that haunted my childhood nightmares, the Twrch Trwyth – but sea-monsters was a step too far. I was surprised that Procopius, an educated and rational man to his roots, believed in such nonsense.

"No, I have not gone mad," he said with the odd, high-pitched cackle that passed for laughter with him, "but I have certain theories as to the origin of these tales, and wish to test them. The crossing of the Strait will provide an ideal opportunity to do so."

"Assuming our fleet is not devoured by Charybdis," I said drily. He laughed again, and threw a bit of bread at me.

Belisarius wasted no time. He had drilled his troops all through the sleepy, peaceful days of summer, keeping them fit and combat-sharp in case our negotiations with the Goths broke down. Now our army was ordered into action at last, and the disparate squadrons of Isaurian archers and spearmen, foederatii troops and bucelarii converged on the port of Messina.

Twelve thousand men, the same number that sailed from Constantinople. Justinian had sent no reinforcements, and expected his golden general to perform the North African miracle all over again. Only this time, Belisarius was ordered to recapture the Roman homeland and her ancient capital, the city of Rome itself.

Thus, with rumbling guts and a sense of foreboding, I boarded Belisarius' flagship once more.

9.

We crossed the narrow Strait with no sign of Homer's sea-monsters, and no resistance from the Goths on the opposite coast. The latter, as Procopius informed me with a knowing look, was due to politics.

"Just yesterday there were five thousand Gothic infantry lining those cliffs," he said, nodding at the rocky coastline of Reggio, "they are all scattered now, thanks to the treachery of their chief, Ebrimur."

"Who is he?" I asked, holding onto the bow for support. The sea-sickness had me in its grip again, and at that moment the prospect of being swallowed up by Charybdis didn't seem so dreadful.

"Theodatus's son-in-law. He put his trust in Ebrimur, but should have known better. The glint of Roman gold overcame the young man's sense of duty, and last night he abandoned his post and took a boat to Sicily. His men woke up to find him gone, and promptly deserted. God grant that all our victories should prove so easy."

Procopius seemed to know a lot about this matter, and it wouldn't have surprised me to learn that he had first suggested to Belisarius that Ebrimur could be bought off. He was much more than just a secretary, as I had discovered at Membresa.

"Presumably Justinian will give the traitor a medal," I said sourly. I was never comfortable with this kind of double-dealing, even though it meant that our army had been spared a battle.

"Much more," said Procopius, "Ebrimur will go to Constantinople, where the Emperor has offered to make him a Patrician and load him down with riches and honours. Such is the reward for treachery."

I spat over the side. "I hope his money brings him comfort. Every right-thinking person will despise him."

Procopius gave a bland little smile, and spoke no more of Ebrimur. The traitor did indeed make his way to the imperial capital, where Justinian received him as a dear friend and gave him all the titles and riches he had been promised. As I predicted, he was held with contempt by everyone else, and died shortly afterwards, possibly murdered. It is best not to rely on the gratitude of emperors.

Our landing at Reggio was unopposed, and the army swiftly formed up into line of march. As in North Africa, Belisarius hugged the coast, with squadrons of cavalry sent ahead as a vanguard and to protect his right flank. The infantry and the baggage toiled along in the rear.

Amid the noise and bustle and summer heat, Procopius somehow found the time to go in search of his monsters, or the truth behind them. Belisarius let him ride out with just one Hunnish horse archer for an escort, even though we were in hostile territory and Procopius was a useful servant.

"Try not to get eaten," I called out as he rode past. In response he treated me to an obscene gesture, which sent a ripple of laughter down the line.

Belisarius and his guards were part of the main body of the army. We rode at a trot, so as not to get too far ahead of the infantry, our banners fluttering in the gentle breeze. The shoreline was immediately to the east, and beyond that the deep blue sea, with our ships strung out on the horizon. As usual, Belisarius had ordered the fleet to shadow the army and remain within sight at all times.

My sickness soon passed, as it always did when I set foot on dry land. I gloried in the fresh air sweeping in from the sea, and the discipline and grandeur of the Roman army on the march.

We marched north through Bruttium in sweltering heat, with the sun beating down mercilessly on our heads and threatening to boil me alive in my heavy coat of mail. The south of Italy was a land of stark contrasts, rocky and arid, but also startlingly beautiful, with emerald green forests and little white-walled towns perched on hills and rocky bluffs.

Belisarius ignored the smaller towns. His objective was Naples, the greatest city in southern Italy, defended by a strong Gothic garrison. The capture of Naples would be a serious blow to Theodatus's prestige, already damaged by his failure to defend Sicily and groveling overtures to Justinian. The reputation of Roman arms also had to be redeemed after our defeat in Dalmatia.

Our army marched through Bruttium and Lucania without encountering any resistance. The native Italians flocked to our standards, hailing us as brothers and deliverers from the oppressive barbarian yoke. This was nonsense: the Goths had governed Italy far better than most of the latter-day Caesars.

The government of Theodatus held to the Arian heresy, which was unpopular in Italy, and his troops had utterly abandoned the countryside. Submitting to Belisarius was the sane and logical decision for the populace to make. Most of the smaller towns lacked adequate defences, and could not have withstood an assault.

Belisarius greeted their adulation and pledges of loyalty with a smiling countenance, and distributed gifts of food and money among the peasants, but his mind was clearly elsewhere. His naturally grave and solemn features became more drawn as we approached Napoli, and I could see the lights in his pavilion burning long into the night. The reduction of Italy's second city represented his greatest challenge since the war against the Vandals. As we marched he kept his eyes fixed on the skyline, watching for any sign of the enemy. It was all far too easy, and no man can roll winning dice forever.

Naples, when we finally arrived within sight of the city walls, was both a formidable obstacle and subject of awe, a vision of ancient Roman splendour and imperial might. Her elegant villas, palaces, temples and aqueducts are graven into my memory, for this was Imperial Rome as I had imagined it as a child in Britain, when my nurse enthralled me with stories of legions and emperors.

In military terms, the city was a nightmare. The land for several miles around had been stripped bare of fodder and livestock by the garrison, and Gothic banners flew defiantly from the ramparts. Like Palermo, Naples was a port, and had no fleet to defend the harbour, but was much better-garrisoned. The Goths inside her walls were crack troops, and unlike the demoralized and ill-trained levies at Palermo would not capitulate after a single bombardment.

"We will have to carry the place by storm," I overheard Bessas say as we surveyed the walls, "or starve them out. And we have no time for a lengthy siege."

There was a note of satisfaction in his voice. Belisarius had described him as an old butcher, and so he was, firmly believing that a victory was hardly worthy of the name unless oceans of blood were spilled. I took one look at Napoli's high walls, lined with rows of gleaming helmets, and the strong iron-bound gates, and shuddered.

Belisarius could not risk any delay, for each day that passed gave the Goths time to gather their strength and ship troops back from Dalmatia. He would have to order an all-out assault, and I would be among those sent up the ladders.

I was also on my guard against further assassination attempts. For reasons I could not fathom, Photius had been left behind in Sicily, though he was expected to join the army eventually. My comrades in the Guards were friendly enough, though I knew at least one had conspired with Photius to try and murder me on the battlefield at Membresa. I was cordial but distant, preferring to mess on my own and discouraging familiarity. Until I knew who the co-conspirator was, I felt unable to trust any of them.

The Neopolitans were as desperate to avoid a slaughter as we were, and persuaded the Goths to allow them to send out a deputation to speak with Belisarius. I stood by the general's side and watched them file out of the city gates, six venerable old men with bald pates and white beards, waving olive branches of peace.

Their spokesmen was named Stephen. He was something of a philosopher and rhetorician, and pleaded eloquently with Belisarius to bypass Napoli and march onto Rome.

"We are true Roman citizens," he declared, flinging out his withered brown hand to indicate the city, "and desire nothing more than to be ruled by a Caesar again."

"Then give up the city," said Belisarius. He was seated at his ease on a chair under an awning, with Antonina curled up beside him on a divan, eating white grapes and eyeing the Neapolitans with amusement.

Her husband made the old men stand, without shelter or refreshment, and wore his stoniest expression. The intention was to impress the ambassadors with his stern and ruthless bearing, and in this he succeeded. The men behind Stephen visibly quailed in the general's presence, and I gave one wrinkled specimen a start by winking at him.

"Alas, the fate of Naples is not in the hands of its people," replied Stephen, "the Goths rule the city, and will not allow us to open the gates. Their merciless king took their wives and children as hostages, and has let it be known that if Naples falls, he will cut all their throats. Therefore, dread Belisarius, you may expect them to fight and die to the last man rather than be conquered."

A groan passed through our officers, but Stephen was not finished. "What benefit," he added with another elaborate flourish, "can ensue to your imperial army from forcing Naples to surrender? Should you march on to Rome, and succeed in capturing her, the whole of Italy shall naturally fall into your hands. The loss of Rome will mean the end of Theodatus, and the families of our garrison here will escape the knife. Should you fail in your attempt on Rome, as is likely, then your capture of Naples shall prove useless, and a vain waste of money and men."

He was blunt, this one, rather too blunt for a diplomat. Belisarius' knuckles went white as he gripped the arms of his chair.

"You are speaking," he said in firm and deliberate tones, "to the victor of Dara and the conqueror of North Africa and Sicily. Every one of my campaigns has been crowned with success."

"Do not mistake that for false modesty, little man. Know that I was sent here by my Emperor to conquer, and so I shall. Do not think to close your gates against an army aiming to win back Italy's freedom, and do not prefer barbarian tyranny to the ancient laws and liberties of Rome."

Stephen began to splutter a protest, but Belisarius stilled his voice with a raised finger. "With regard to the Gothic soldiers, I offer them a choice. They may either enlist in my army, and share in our exploits and rewards, or they are free to disband and return to their homes. The fate of their families is not in my hands, except to say that I would disdain to serve a king who makes such craven threats against women and children. Persuade them to surrender, and I swear that your lives and properties shall go untouched."

Stephen glumly shook his head, and so they prosed on for hours, arguing back and forth while the sun slowly dipped beyond the western hills and cramp stole into my aching limbs.

It was all a game, of course. For all his seeming virtue, Stephen was rotten to the core, and easily corrupted. When the official conference was over, he was invited to dinner with Belisarius and Antonina, and over the main course offered a huge bribe in gold and silver to stir up unrest inside Naples. He acquiesced, and returned the following morning with his fellows, no longer a servant of the Goths, but a double agent in the employ of Rome.

His efforts had no immediate effect, and for several days we sat and waited for the gates to swing open and admit us. Belisarius had a tight grip on the city, having invested it by land and sea. Nothing could leave or enter without his knowledge.

The Gothic soldiers on the battlements threw defiance at us, beating their spears on their shield and mocking us for robbers and degenerates, boy-lovers and stunted Easterlings and I know not what else. They had every reason to be confident. Our twelve thousand men must have looked a poor and scanty host, against the many thousands of Goths mustering in the north.

Theodatus, however, with all the advantages at his disposal, did nothing. He was a coward, and refused to lead his troops to relieve Naples, or send another man in his stead.

During this time Procopius returned, none the worse for his little adventure. I approached him after he had made his report to Belisarius, and asked how his quest for legendary monsters had fared.

"Success, I think," he said, slapping his thin hands together, "an age-old mystery is solved."

I gave him a cynical look, and he laughed. "No monsters, Coel. Scylla the six-headed hydra is nothing more than a rugged outcrop of rock, part of a cliff on the Italian side of the Strait. In darkness and foul weather, it is easy to understand how fearful sailors might have mistaken the outcrop for some kind of monster."

"What of Charybdis, the ship-swallowing demon?"

"A whirlpool, I suspect, off the coast of Sicily. Both natural elements are within arrow-shot of each other, so they quickly became merged in legend. When I have time, I will write down my findings and present them to the imperial court in Constantinople."

I glanced outside the pavilion, at the high walls of Naples and the peaceful city that lay beyond them, apparently undisturbed by the presence of our army without.

"If any of us ever see Constantinople again," I said gloomily, "unless our agents do their work, Belisarius will waste his strength outside this city. At some point Theodatus must find his courage, or the Goths will put him aside and choose a braver chief."

Belisarius was always careful of the lives of his men, and reluctant to throw them away in a frontal assault on Naples. The city was protected by steep ground on the landward side, and any attempt to storm the harbour would end in catastrophe: the garrison had learned from the example of Palermo, and stocked their ramparts with war-machines to guard against any approach by our ships.

Bessas and the other officers demanded that an attempt be made to storm the walls, and at last Belisarius yielded. In the early hours of morning, just before first light, he sent in his Isaurian infantry, supported by detachments of foederatii, with ladders and grapples to scale the ramparts near the eastern gate.

The Goths were waiting for them. I stood and watched the slaughter, muffled up in a heavy cloak against the morning chill and privately thanking God that Belisarius had kept his guards in reserve.

Our men stormed up the slope, arrows and javelins hurled from the battlements clattering against their upraised shields. Many fell, but more reached the foot of the walls and swarmed up the ladders. Hard fighting followed, and I sensed Belisarius' tension as the struggle for the ramparts swayed back and forth. Spears and axes glinted in the morning mist, and the clatter of steel mingled with the screams and shouts of the combatants.

"Sheer folly," I heard him mutter, "I have sacrificed my men on the altar of vanity. God forgive me."

The assault failed. Our men lacked the numbers, while the Goths were continually reinforced from inside. Belisarius held his head in dismay as the Isaurians broke and fled back down the ladders and ropes, pursued by the jeers of the enemy and a storm of missiles. They left the slope carpeted with dead and dying. In a single assault we lost above three hundred men, far more than we could afford.

Bessas and Troglita urged another assault the following day, but Belisarius would not hear of it. He returned to his pavilion to brood and accept what comfort his wife could give him. Always, in times of grief and difficulty, he resorted to Antonina. That was where her power lay.

The vital days of autumn slid away, and still our army languished hopelessly outside Naples. Unknown to us, Stephen's efforts to whip the citizens into revolt had been blocked by two of his fellow rhetoricians, named Pastor and Asclepiodotus, both of whom were devoted to the Gothic cause. Inspired by these, the people threw in their lot with the Goths, and joined with them in haughtily commanding us to withdraw.

Procopius buried himself in the histories of Italy, which he had brought to him from strong-rooms and libraries all over Lucania. Belisarius appeared to have no need of him. With no reinforcements on hand, and nothing save bad advice from his captains, the general sank into a torpor.

With defeat grinning at us, I thought this a bad time for Procopius to give himself up to scholarly pursuits, and told him so.

"You look tired, Coel," he replied, looking up from a yellowing scroll he had been studying, "you should get more rest."

"I will rest, when I know I can lay my head down at night without fear of an assassin's blade. What is that rag of old sheepskin you're peering at?"

He rested his chin on his knuckles and smiled at me. "A history of Naples during the reign of Augustus," he replied, "it is extremely dull, and badly-written, but useful."

"Here," he said, peeling back the scroll and placing his thumb on another beneath it, "is a crude diagram of the Aqua Augusta, as mapped out by Roman architects."

I squinted at the faint lines on the decayed bit of parchment. They showed the lines of a great aqueduct constructed during Augustus's reign, some five hundred years previously.

"The aqueduct was intended to supply fresh water to no less than eight Roman cities in the Bay of Naples," said Procopius, "including Naples, of course. Eight cities! A staggering achievement, but one the Romans of old were capable of performing. Its source was the mountains outside the city of Avellino in Campania."

"I have seen the ruins of the aqueduct," I said, "some stretches remain, scattered around Naples. What of it?"

Procopius sat back in his chair. "You are on light duties at present, are you not?" he asked.

I wondered at his sudden change of subject. "Belisarius has little need of me, other than my shifts guarding his pavilion."

"Good. Then you have plenty of free time to improve your mind. We are in the heart of Italy, Coel! The centre of the

Western Empire, before it fell to pieces. There is so much you can learn here."

"I'm not much of a scholar," I said, eyeing him warily. Procopius seldom indulged in idle chat.

"I certainly cannot imagine you devoting yourself to study," he said, "the hard-faced British warrior, spending his days staring at ancient writings? No, you are of a more practical disposition. I think you should explore some of the ruins of the Aqua Augusta."

He plucked a scroll from the heap, scanned it quickly, and held it out to me. "There is a particularly interesting series of channels sketched out here," he said, "a little to the west of the city. Go and seek them out, Coel, and marvel at the wonders of Roman architecture."

10.

I did as Procopius suggested, and rode out that same afternoon to inspect the remains of the aqueduct west of Naples, less than a mile from the boundaries of our camp.

Seen close to, the ruins of the Aqua Augusta were a great crumbling series of stone arches piled on top of each other, ivy-grown and decayed, and in places entirely fallen away. Part of the channel was still connected to the city, but there were gaps in the rows of arches above the surface. The surrounding land was a wet and stagnant bog, thanks to the water seeping out of the disused channel and polluting the ground.

I tethered my horse in a little wood and wandered among the ruins. The complexities of the design were beyond me, but I knew that the majority of the wells and cisterns were underground.

"There will be entrances to these subterranean tunnels," Procopius told me before I left, "find one, and explore as far as you may. I trust you have no fear of dark, constricted spaces."

In fact I did, but it seemed to unwise to say so. Procopius had sent me here with more than mere sightseeing in mind.

The ruins were silent. No birds sang nearby, and I began to feel I had entered a mausoleum. The Aqua Augusta had once been a glory of the Empire, but like the Empire it had fallen into neglect and disrepair. I was an ant, a pygmy, wandering haplessly through the remnants of a dead civilization.

At last I found a narrow rent in the wall, once a doorway, but partially blocked up by fallen masonry. It was still wide enough for me to squeeze through. For some time I stood irresolute, contemplating the darkness that lay beyond with fear and trepidation. My skin crawled at the thought of groping through the shadows beneath the earth, and of what might be lurking in those long-abandoned tunnels.

Turn back, or press on. Some residual sense of duty overturned my fear, and I scraped though the gap.

Beyond was a passage, wide enough for two men, and a stone floor that sloped sharply downwards. Gulping down a sense of panic, I shuffled carefully down the passage, keeping one hand pressed against the damp wall. The floor was slimy, but my way was guided by the light streaming through the entrance.

The light was snuffed out as I descended further. For a time I crept along in total darkness. The air was musty and warm. All was silence, save for the steady drip-drip of water somewhere close by. My breathing came hard and fast, and my heart fluttered in my chest like a trapped bird.

At any moment I felt certain the walls would close in, forcing me into a steadily shrinking space, until I was crushed inside a stone box. I almost soiled myself at the prospect of being buried alive in this dreadful vault. Only the reassuring weight of Caledfwlch at my hip prevented me from turning back.

Blessed light returned, slanting through collapsed sections of the ceiling, far above my head. I found myself following a steadily widening passage. An arched channel, similar to the ones I had seen above ground, ran through the middle of the passage and vanished into the darkness ahead. It was smaller than the surface arches, about eight feet high and four wide. I was no engineer, but even I could see that the water that supplied Naples had once flowed along the conduit.

The passage was not straight, but ran in crooked lines for what seemed like several miles. I followed it for as far as my courage would take me. My nerves were stretched to breaking point, when the passage came to a sudden end.

I was confronted by a wall of natural rock, pierced by an aperture wide enough for water to flow on into the remainder of the passage beyond and into the city. Heart thumping, I climbed up onto the lip of the channel and peered along the gap. It was too narrow for a man to pass through, but the rock was soft here, and could be widened by picks.

Excitement swelled inside me. Here was a secret route into the city.

I carefully dropped back onto the floor. It was vital I returned to Belisarius at once, and informed him of this unlooked-for doorway to Naples.

Not unlooked-for: Procopius must have suspected its existence from his studies, and sent me to search for it.

My fear of dark and enclosed spaces lifted as I ran back down the passage, replaced by glorious visions of being publicly fêted as a hero, the man who saved Belisarius from almost certain defeat. He would be grateful, that was certain, and perhaps even give me a command. I pictured myself at the head of a troop of cavalry, proud mailed lancers on good horses, and knew that Arthur's shade would be proud of me.

I stopped dead. Some echo had reached my ears, a snatch of whispered conversation, quickly stifled. It drifted from somewhere up ahead, the dark stretch of passage which no light could reach.

There it was again:

"You should not have come…"

This was a man's voice, deep and low.

"I had to. I wanted to see his face. Once more…"

A woman's voice this time, with an awful familiarity about it that made me shiver. It could not be. My mind was playing tricks, or else the ghosts of my past had somehow found a voice in this subterranean hell.

The voices were stilled, but then I heard footsteps, very faint, but definitely there. Someone – no, two people – were trying to move quietly, but the echo was defeating their efforts.

I pressed my back flat against the wall. My mouth had dried up. Terror clouded my thoughts.

Antonina had sent her murderers after me. Was that the true reason for Procopius sending me here, alone, where I could be quietly killed and my body disposed of? Had he betrayed me? Did I have no true friends in this world?

I forced myself to be calm. The sound of footsteps was getting louder. If they were assassins, they were careless about their work. Over-confidence, perhaps. The presence of a woman puzzled me. Female assassins were not unknown, but the butchering of an armed soldier in the dark was work for men.

"Once more…"

Those words replayed in my mind. I had a suspicion of who had uttered them, and it tore at my heart. Still, she had betrayed me once, so why not again?

I looked around desperately for a hiding place. The conduit inside the channel was the most obvious. I would have preferred a recess in the wall, but there was none. The walls of the passage stretched away either of me, smooth and flat and featureless.

"See, here are his marks…"

The man's voice again. He had discovered my footprints. I clambered up the arch in front of me, gritting my teeth as I scraped my wrists and ankles on the rough stone. There were plenty of handholds, and I quickly scrambled up and over into the dry conduit, where I lay flat on my back. I slowly drew Caledfwlch and laid the blade across my chest, ready to use.

Now their steps were right beneath me. I could hear their breathing: rapid, heavy, the sound of people in fear. That was some comfort. These were no cool, ruthless killers, but novices, every bit as nervous and frightened as their prey.

It would have been easy to remain hidden, but my soul revolted against being stalked like an animal. I had the advantage, not they, and would use it.

I turned on my side and peered over the channel. Two people were almost directly under me. The light was dim, but I could see one was a slender woman with glossy black hair flowing to her shoulders, and her companion a heavily-built man in the scale mail and crested helmet of the Guards.

I silently leaped over the edge and dropped down onto the guardsman. He folded under me, and together we went down in a tangle of limbs and curses.

He dropped his sword, but was sharp enough to seize my wrist instead of trying to retrieve it. His helmet had also come loose. I smashed my knee into his face, felt bone crunch against bone, and clawed at his eyes with my free hand. The guardsman's companion might have helped him, but instead she took to her heels.

I was the stronger, and managed to get on top of him, my left forearm pressed down on his windpipe.

Now I could see his face. He was indeed a Guard, though I didn't know his name. I had seen him in drills and on the march, though he always kept his distance. We had never spoken.

I eased the pressure on his windpipe a little. "Why do you hunt me?" I demanded. His fingers on my wrist had slackened, and I threatened him with Caledfwlch, holding the tip a mere half-inch from his right eye.

His eyes were full of fear, but he made no answer. "Come," I said, "I cannot believe Antonina inspires such loyalty. You are in her pay, are you not? Would you truly die for her?"

Still no answer. I recalled that Antonina inspired terror in her followers. A man in her service would rather die a quick death at the point of a blade, rather than suffer the penalties she inflicted for failure.

The running footsteps of his companion were dying away. If I tarried much longer, she would have made good her escape.

"Well," I said regretfully, "it seems a pity."

He tried to jerk his head away, but I seized him by the throat and stabbed Caledfwlch into his eye. The blade slid easily into his brain, killing him almost instantly. His body stiffened under me and went still.

Leaving him, I got up and ran down the passage, plunging into darkness and emerging at the bottom of the sloping floor that led up to the entrance. The shadow of my quarry flitted ahead of me, and was briefly silhouetted in the narrow opening as her slender form darted through into daylight.

I pounded up the slope, breath rasping in my throat, and squeezed through the gap. Flinging up a hand to shield my eyes against the glare of the sun, I stumbled outside, looking around for my quarry.

There she was, tearing feverishly at the bridle of her horse, a fine grey cavalry mount, tethered to a crumbling pillar of rock. My heart stopped as I recognized her.

"Elene," I cried out, "you cannot run from me. Not forever."

She threw a terrified glance over her shoulder. Yes, Elene, the first woman I had loved and lain with. Still the same lithe, sinuous creature I knew at the Hippodrome, though she must have been nearing forty by now, with the occasional streak of grey in her long, unbound black hair.

She wore a grey tunic of grey silk, tucked in at the waist, and loose breeches. A dagger hung from a brown leather sheath at her hip. A second horse, another cavalry beast, was tethered next to hers. This one had clearly belonged to her dead companion.

I started towards her, but she had already swung gracefully into the saddle. Elene had learned to sit astride a horse, like a man, at the arena.

She turned her pony's head away, but hesitated for a moment, looking directly at me. Her long face had lost its youthful bloom, and was now gaunt and tired, the face of one who had wandered too far down dark roads.

I groped for something to say. I was almost certain that she and her accomplice had stalked me in the tunnel with the intention of murdering me, but I didn't want her to flee and vanish from my life again, not yet.

"Your son," I said, "does he live?"

I had last seen Elene in the cells under the Praetorium in Constantinople, where she had tried to persuade me to confess to conspiring with the Nika rioters. She did so, she claimed, on the orders of the Empress Theodora, who had threatened to kill her husband and little son if she refused.

Elene had also claimed that the boy was named Arthur in honour of me, even though he was another man's get. I doubted the tale, thinking it a cruel joke to hurt me, but had pondered it much in the years since. Perhaps there was a son after all. Perhaps she had lied to her husband about the paternity. Elene would have become a practiced liar in the service of Theodora.

She swallowed hard, and pushed back a strand of black hair from her eyes. These were as I remembered them, grey and tinged with a strange melancholy.

"My son is none of your affair," she replied huskily, "you will not speak of him. Where is Lucius?"

Lucius, the man I had killed. I noted his name and stored it away for future enquiry. "Dead," I replied brutally, "I left him to rot in the shadows, as he deserves."

A terrible thought occurred to me. "Was he your lover – your husband?"

For the first time in many years I heard Elene laugh. "No. Merely a man I was obliged to work with. Farewell, Coel. I will see you again, before you die."

She turned her pony's head and heeled the beast into a gallop. I ran for my own horse, tethered in the wood outside the ruins, but stopped. There was no point in pursuing Elene. Her pony was fast, and would have outdistanced mine even in a fair race.

I swore, and thumped the wall. Elene had escaped me again.

11.

Procopius made a great show of shock and outrage when I told him of the attempt on my life. I carefully searched his face as he paced about his tent, cursing and shaking his fist, and concluded his anger was genuine.

"Belisarius must not know of it," I said when he had calmed down, "Elene and Lucius were almost certainly in the service of Antonina."

"I know, I know," he replied, suddenly weary, and sat down beside his writing desk, "this is my fault. They must have been watching you. I should have sent you out with an armed guard, but that might have drawn attention."

"There are two Huns, lying dead somewhere near Membresa, who had cause to regret guarding me," I replied.

"God or the Devil must be watching over you," he said, shaking his head, "that is twice now your enemies have tried and failed. There will be a third attempt, I am sure of it."

I shrugged, trying to give the impression that I cared nothing for assassins, though in truth I was badly scared. "I am alive, and unharmed, and one of their hired killers lies dead. Let them try."

Procopius closed his eyes for a few seconds and pinched the bridge of his hooked nose. Then he was all business again.

"This aperture you found," he said, turning to the scrolls laid out flat on his desk, "at the end of the old channel that leads into Naples. Show me exactly where it is."

His maps of the aqueduct were very old, stained with damp and moth-eaten in many places, but I managed to trace my route through the tunnels. Procopius stared at the parchment, nodding slightly and tapping his chin.

"Come," he said suddenly, rolling up the parchment, "Belisarius must be told."

We made our way to the general's pavilion, where we found Belisarius sitting outside under a tree and staring at the walls of Naples. Other than two of his guards, he was alone. Antonina was absent with her ladies-in-waiting, no doubt amusing herself somewhere.

He greeted us with his usual courtesy, but was in a pensive mood, and clearly in no mood for conversation. His mood swiftly lightened as I told him of my adventure – excluding the murder attempt, of course – and discovery of a secret way into the city.

"Can it be true?" he exclaimed, staring at me with desperate hope in his eyes. Procopius showed him the fragment of map charting out the route of the underground aqueduct west of Naples.

Belisarius, for so long a frustrated and disappointed figure, instantly recovered his old self. "Summon Bessas, Troglita and Photius to my pavilion," he ordered one of his guards, "they are to come as soon as possible."

I exchanged glances with Procopius. "Photius is here, sir?" I asked, striving to keep the emotion out of my voice.

Belisarius was striding about, rubbing his hands together, his brows knitted in thought. "What?" he said distractedly, "Photius? Yes, he is here. Sicily is quiet, so I summoned him to join us with as many men as he could spare. He came with a hundred or so. Not enough, but a hundred is better than none."

I racked my brain for an excuse to withdraw. I could not face Photius, not here in the open, not now. The blood pounded in my veins as I contemplated setting eyes on the treacherous pig. How could I, in all honour, restrain myself from plunging Caledfwlch into his heart? Murder committed in the broad light of day, in front of so many witnesses, could not go unpunished, and the old line of British princes would end in hemp.

Procopius appreciated the difficulty. His mind was quicker than mine, and came up with a solution.

"Go and fetch the rest of the scrolls from my tent, Coel," he ordered me, "I think there are some duplicate maps of the aqueduct among them."

The implication was clear: make yourself scarce, and don't come back until the council is over. I gratefully withdrew, and waited nervously in Procopius' tent until he returned some hours later.

"Belisarius was annoyed at your failure to return," he said, yawning, "but I persuaded him that the duplicates weren't necessary, thank God. There are none anyway."

"So what was decided?" I asked.

"He is going to send a detachment of Isaurians into the tunnel. They will widen the aperture, until it is large enough to admit men in full armour, and then offer the Neapolitans a final opportunity to surrender. If they refuse…Naples will suffer the horrors of the sack."

"Was my name mentioned during the council?"
"It was. Belisarius spoke highly of you, and I had the pleasure of seeing young Photius' face drain of blood. His mother must have informed him that you are still alive, but still he was shocked to hear your name on the general's lips. And frightened, if I am any judge."

That was something. Photius now knew that I stood even higher in the favour of Belisarius, which might dissuade him from trying another clumsy attempt on my life. I decided that his mother was responsible for sending Lucius and Elene to hunt me in the tunnels below the aqueduct. Unless Procopius had indeed betrayed me - which I doubted, considering the efforts he had made on my behalf – she must have had spies watching my movements.

I groaned. More traitors in the Guards, perhaps, or among Belisarius' staff. It was impossible to be certain. All I could do was live from day to day, guard my back, and pray my luck held.

The next day Belisarius sent heralds to the gates of Naples, summoning Stephen and the elders of the city to his presence once more. They shuffled outside and, as before, met Belisarius at his pavilion.

Stephen looked drawn and ill with terror, as well he might, since his efforts to raise the citizens of Naples against their Gothic overlords had proved futile. Belisarius had paid a lot of gold for his useless services, and he must have feared that the general meant to take his head as recompense.

Belisarius calmed his fears by embracing him as a brother. "I have a message," he said, holding the quaking old man at arm's length, "that I wish you to remember and repeat to your fellow citizens. It is this."

He stepped back and flung up his right arm in a grand flourish, aping the rhetorician's pompous, old-fashioned style in a way that drew a chuckle from his officers.

"I have often seen cities taken by storm," he boomed, "and know too well, from experience, the sad results which commonly ensue. In the memory of these I view, as in a mirror, the future fate of Naples, and my compassion is strongly moved at its impending ruin. I frankly tell you that I have prepared an expedient for entering your walls, of which the success is certain. It would fill me with grief if so ancient and noble a city, peopled by brother Christians and Romans, suffered the havoc of war, and especially by an army under my command. My authority would be insufficient to restrain the victorious troops from bloodshed and pillage; they partly consist of barbarians, who claim no kinship with Rome, and would regard your downfall without pain. During the short respite I have granted you, while it is still in your power to deliberate and choose, prefer, I beseech you, your own safety, and avoid the destruction hovering over you. Should you reject my offers, you may blame the sufferings that follow, not on my desire for vengeance or the harshness of fortune, but to your own stubborn folly."

It was a powerful speech, in a style calculated to appeal to the scholars and rhetoricians inside Naples, as well as strike terror into the citizens.

Stephen bowed. "I shall tell them, General Belisarius," he murmured, his face ashen, "I shall tell them to prefer life over death."

The deputation returned to Naples and recited Belisarius' threats to the populace, to no avail. The Neapolitans and the Goths still held us in contempt, and were convinced that Theodatus would soon send an army to chase us away.

Belisarius' patience was at an end. Even as he spoke with Stephen, his Isaurians were at work under the aqueduct, widening the aperture I had found at the end of the channel.

It was dusk by the time the Isaurians returned. Belisarius now ordered four hundred men, led by myself and an officer named Magnus, to make our way to the tunnel and prepare to attack. We were provided with dark cloaks, covered lanterns to light our way, and two trumpeters to sound the signal when we broke into the city.

"When we hear the trumpets outside, I will order a general assault on the walls," Belisarius informed us at a last hurried council, "Bessas and the pick of my troops will scale the ramparts, while you storm through the streets and open the gates from the inside to admit the rest of our men. Understood?"

I and the cluster of officers around me murmured in agreement. Photius was among them, and I could feel his eyes scorching into my back. I refused to look at him, fearing that my temper would overflow.

"Control yourself," Procopius had advised me before hand, "do not lunge at your enemies, but be content to wait. Your opportunity for revenge will come."

That opportunity, I had decided, would arise during the sack of Naples. When the fighting was at its hottest in the streets, amid the chaos and bloodshed, I would stalk Photius like a tiger might stalk its prey in the jungle.

Our assault very nearly met with disaster. Magnus and his four hundred men followed me to the ruins of the aqueduct, where I managed to find the entrance again after some witless stumbling about. There, to my amazement, at least half of his command refused to enter the tunnels.

"I will not go through that portal," declared one of the faint hearts, "it is a doorway to Hell."

Magnus raged at them, but they would not be moved, and in the end it was only the arrival of Belisarius in person that restored the situation.

"What is the reason for this delay?" he demanded, his face pale with fury, "into the tunnels at once, you laggards, or I will have every tenth man among you executed by his fellows!" The threat of decimation, an ancient punishment not used in the Roman army for centuries, was enough to restore their courage.

Once again I descended that sloping floor into pitch darkness, though this time I had the comfort of a lantern and hundreds of men at my back. While I retraced my steps through the subterranean passage, Bessas and his detachment advanced towards the foot of the rampart above ground.

Soon we reached the end of the channel, and caught a glimpse of starry night sky through the gap in the wall that the Isaurians had mined and widened.

I paused to study the gap. The path through it led upwards into a courtyard, at a steep incline that would be difficult for a man in armour to ascend.

"I will go first," I whispered to Magnus, "give me a rope, and I will drop it down for the next man to follow."

He agreed, and I stripped off my helm and coat of mail. I weighed Caledfwlch in my hand before handing it over to Magnus for safe keeping. As ever, I was reluctant to place my precious heirloom in the hands of another, especially a stranger.

In the end I decided to risk the extra weight, and slung my sword-belt over my shoulder. Magnus and another soldier boosted me up the wall, and I clung to the almost sheer sides like a monkey, groping for handholds.

Straining with effort, I struggled upwards by inches, Caledfwlch dangling awkwardly down my back. Somehow I scrambled up and over the edge of the hole, and threw myself, panting, onto the cobbles of the courtyard.

When I had recovered my breath, I got up and approached the large olive tree in the middle of the yard, meaning to tie the rope around the trunk and pay it down the gap for the next man.

"Who goes there? What are you doing? Intruders! Help! Murder!"

A woman's voice, shrill and cracked and elderly, squawked behind me. I let out an involuntary yelp and spun around. Caledfwlch banged against my thigh as I scrabbled for the hilt, though I was faced with nothing more formidable than a fat old peasant woman in a brown smock and an apron dusted with flour.

Nothing more formidable, did I say? She had a broad, lantern-jawed face, and stuck out her chin as I finally managed to wrestle Caledfwlch free of its sheath.

"Brave young man," she sneered, folding her heavy forearms, "to draw sword against a woman. Come near me with that thing, sir, and I will scream for help. I have neighbours who will hear me."

She was a problem I failed to foresee. I had assumed the house that adjoined the courtyard, being in such a ruinous state, was deserted.

What could I do? Bessas would have put his sword through her heart, without hesitation, but I wasn't made of such stern metal.

Procopius would have appreciated the absurdity of the situation. The entire fate of our assault on Naples, and on the Italian campaign in general, now depended on me silencing one querulous old matron.

"Please," I said in a wheedling voice, "remain silent, and you shall be amply rewarded."

She raised one hairy eyebrow. "Rewarded, eh? Rewarded by whom, may I ask? You speak with a strange accent. I think you are one of General Belisarius' foreign mercenaries, come to murder us all while we sleep. I'll not have it!"

She started to suck in a deep breath. Before she could scream, I dived at her and struck out with Caledfwlch. The flat of the blade whipped across her face with a noise like a wet cloth slapping against rock. Her little eyes crossed, and with a gentle sigh she folded into a heap.

God forgive me, I had struck a woman. Cruel necessity demanded it, yet still I made the sign of the cross before sheathing Caledfwlch and hurrying back to the olive tree. My fingers shook with nervous excitement as I took the coil of rope from my belt, looped and made it fast round the narrow trunk, and tossed the other end down the gap.

We worked with feverish haste, but something like two hours had passed before all our men were lifted to the surface. I retrieved my armour and struggled back into it. As for my matron, she was trussed and gagged and safely deposited in a corner of the yard, where she struggled in vain and none molested her.

A good portion of the night remained, and the first grey shreds of dawn were yet to pierce the night sky. "To the gates," said Magnus, "Bessas will be waiting."

The broken-down timber gate of the courtyard opened onto a narrow alleyway. We crept down it, two by two, four hundred men attempting to move as silently as mice. Procopius had shown us his old maps of the city, so we had some vague idea of our location, and that we had to make our way to the gatehouse on the northern wall.

Naples slept soundly. The streets were deserted, and nothing opposed our progress save a couple of stray dogs, who barked indignantly at us until I heaved a rock at them. The curs loped away down a side-street, and we continued on to the gatehouse.

When the twin towers flanking the gate rose before us, Magnus ordered a dozen men forward to deal with the Gothic sentinels on the rampart.

I was one of the dozen. We removed our boots, and ran noiselessly on bare feet across the cobbles and up the steps. The guards drowsed at their posts, and didn't sense our approach until we were on them. I slid my arm around a brawny Gothic neck and drew the edge of my dagger across his throat. He writhed and kicked in my grip, gasping for air as blood pumped from the gash. I threw him off the parapet, and his flailing body hit the cobbles like a sack of meal.

The rest of our men were quick and silent about their work, and within seconds four Goths lay dead. Our trumpeters raised their instruments to their lips. The shrill blasts echoed across the darkened plain beyond, and were answered by a roar from Bessas' men. They had crawled as close as they dared to the foot of the walls, and laid flat on their bellies, waiting for the signal to attack. Now the plain seemed to come alive as they sprang to their feet and rushed the gates.

Somewhere a gong sounded, and lights flared in the street below. Gothic soldiers stumbled from the guardrooms flanking the gates, still half-asleep as they buckled on shields and helmets, shouting blearily at each other in their strange tongue. Magnus and the rest of our men burst out of hiding and quickly overwhelmed them. A brutal street-brawl broke out, figures grappling with each other in darkness.

War-horns sounded. I looked to my left, and saw a file of Goths storming along the parapet towards us. Big men, as they tend to be, with long fair hair spilling over their mailed shoulders. Their axes were huge, double-handed butcher's tools, capable of cleaving a man in half.

I was the officer present, and the Isaurians who had slaughtered the sentinels looked to me for orders. The axe-men were a terrifying prospect, but I didn't dare show cowardice in front of the men.

"Stand your ground," I shouted, drawing Caledfwlch and advancing to meet the leading Goth. The parapet was narrow, barely wide enough for two men abreast, and he filled the space with his enormous bulk.

I remember him vividly: well over six feet of solid bone and muscle, an officer or nobleman, with a heavy green cloak thrown back over his broad shoulders, fastened with an elaborate golden brooch in the shape of a leaping stag. His mail was of superb quality, shining like a mirror in the pale moonlight, and his yellow moustaches and plaited beard flowed to his breast.

All these details stuck in my mind, even though I had little time to study the brute before he sprang at me, snarling and whirling his axe.

He was fearsomely strong, but slow. I dodged aside and that terrible axe, which must have carried twenty pounds of steel in the head, swept past and dashed against the stonework with a terrific clang.

My back was against the wall. I thrust at his face, missed, and Caledfwlch scraped harmlessly against his armoured shoulder. The axe rose again, his blue eyes glinted in triumph, and then a throwing knife sprouted from his neck like some obscene plant.

He dropped his axe and clawed at the blade, buried almost to the hilt in his flesh, gasping for breath as blood flowed down his fingers. I placed my foot against his chest and heeled him off the walkway. He vanished over the edge, but another Goth rushed at me before I could thank the knife-thrower.

I closed with the Goth before he could strike, seizing the haft of his axe and stabbing wildly at his face and eyes. Somehow his helm worked loose in the struggle, and I accidentally butted him on the nose. My eyes watered in pain, he threw his arms around me, and for a second or two we teetered on the edge. It was a twenty-foot drop or more to the cobbles below.

Desperation lent me an edge in strength. I managed to push him away and rammed my knee into his crotch. He grunted and doubled over, and my heart nearly stopped as an Isaurian leaped out of nowhere, screaming like a devil, and buried his hatchet in the back of the Goth's skull.

"Good work," I panted, helping the Isaurian to shove the dying Goth back against his comrades. They retreated a few steps, and had to push him off the parapet before advancing again.

I stood ready to meet them, but then the gates burst open below us and our infantry stormed into the city. Magnus's men had unbarred the gates from within. At the same time Bessas and his chosen men scaled the walls – I learned later that their attack was delayed by the ladders being too short, and they had to bind two together to make the ascent – and flooded onto the rampart, bawling war-cries.

Now the city would suffer for her arrogance. The remainder of that night was a massacre. Our soldiers ran wild in the streets, slaughtering and burning and pillaging as they pleased. All their pent-up rage and frustration was unleashed, and there was nothing Belisarius or his captains could do to bring the men back under control. The Goths abandoned the walls and tried to stage a fighting retreat to the governor's palace, but our men hunted them like dogs.

The Hunnish mercenaries in particular excelled in savagery. They tore the Goths apart, dipped their hands into still-warm bodies and daubed their faces with hot blood. Unlike the rest of our soldiers, they had no respect or veneration for God, and stripped the altars of churches, murdering those priests who bravely tried to resist them.

Of the citizens, only the Jews put up any form of resistance. They had been foremost in resisting our previous failed assaults, and despaired of receiving any mercy from Belisarius. He would have forgiven them, as he forgave almost everyone who asked it of him. Alas, they assumed he was a monster, and fought to the last.

More than one Roman officer also indulged in looting, and made his fortune from the plundered wealth of Naples. I might have joined them, but my mind was enflamed with desire for revenge on Photius. I prowled the streets, ignoring the murder and riot and rape going on all around me, my mind as sharp and focused as any predator's.

I knew Photius had been among the main body of our men waiting outside the gates. After the Gothic resistance was crushed, they had dispersed, and so he might be anywhere in the city. I silently begged God to lead me to him, but my pleas went unheard. For hours I hunted in vain, until the screams of the dying and the crackle of burning buildings ebbed a little, and the arrival of morning cast pale, sickly light on a scene of total destruction.

Belisarius rode into the city at the head of a hundred Guards, and did his best to restore a semblance of order and discipline. Our men were scattered all over the city, drunk on slaughter and stolen wine. A number of captives had been taken by the Huns, mostly women and children. Belisarius had to negotiate with the Hunnish officers, as though they were equals rather than subordinates, to persuade them to release the captives unharmed.

I had long since given up my hopeless quest, and slumped to rest under the awning of a pillaged wine-shop. Procopius found me here, picking his way delicately over the pieces of smashed vases and amphoras that littered the street, and the slumbering bodies of Isaurian bowmen.

"Coel," he yelled, shaking me awake, "get up, man. Are you sober? If so, Belisarius should have you stuffed and mounted as a rare exhibit."

He peeled one of my eyelids open, but I pushed him away. "Yes, I'm sober," I said irritably, "let me alone. I need to sleep. Photius escaped me."

Procopius sat back on his meatless haunches. "I know. I saw him at the general's pavilion this morning, sharing breakfast with his mother. They seemed in high spirits."

I got up, wincing at the aches and pains in my body, reminding me that I was no longer young. "No doubt they are hatching some new plot," I said, yawning and stretching until the joints in my shoulders clicked, "some fresh way of putting me in the earth."

"You flatter yourself, Coel. Antonina and her son have a great many enemies. You are merely an irritant, an insect to be stamped on when the occasion presents itself."

"An insect? My thanks. It is good to know one's true worth."

I was starving, but Procopius had thought to bring a loaf of bread, and I gnawed at it as we made our way through the reeking streets towards the palace.

Corpses lay everywhere, bloating like dead cattle in the wan morning sun. Flies buzzed about them, and the stench of blood and death and smoke hung over the city like a vile cloud.

The gates of the palace were shut, and the remainder of the Gothic garrison had barricaded themselves inside.

"Eight hundred remain in arms," said Procopius, "Belisarius has surrounded the palace with as many troops as he could find that were reasonably sober and could stand upright, but so far the Goths have refused his entreaties."

I paused, squinting up at the palace, a large rectangular complex built in the typical Roman style, comprising four wings with colonnaded fronts, arranged in a square. A double line of Huns and Isaurians were drawn up in front of the main gates. Many were still suffering from the previous night's excesses, and stood slackly to attention, leaning heavily on their spears.

Bessas was in command, but there was no sign of Belisarius. "The general was called away," he said, "some of the citizens have gone mad, and are demanding the deaths of Pastor and Asclepiodotus."

These two were the rhetoricians who had inspired the citizens to stay loyal to the Goths. Now the fickle mass of the people, who had listened to their advice and hailed them as wise men and patriots, were turning on them.

"They will be torn to pieces," I said carelessly, stifling another yawn, "unless Belisarius reaches them in time. What about Stephen and the others we bribed?"

"In hiding," replied Bessas, "or fled, I know not which, nor do I care. The fate of traitors is of no interest to me."

Belisarius returned wearing his most severe expression, jaw clenched, eyes glittering with rage.

"Murdered in the street," he said in answer to our unspoken queries, "they caught Asclepiodotus as he tried to flee the city in disguise, and ripped him limb from limb. By the time I arrived, they were parading his head on a spear."

He paused to spit. "Savages. I should have the lot of them hanged."

That was impossible. Our invasion of Italy was supposed to be a war of liberation rather than conquest, a grand attempt to snatch back the Roman homeland from the dominion of barbarians. These same Roman citizens, who had refused to open their gates to us, thrown in their lot with the Goths and murdered a defenceless old man, were the people we had come to rescue.

The evidence of our failure was all around us, in the smoking rubble of Naples and the hundreds of citizens abused, robbed and slaughtered at the hands of our soldiers. Belisarius could not resort to hanging people, even if they were murderers, without further exposing the hypocrisy of our cause.

"What of Pastor?" asked Procopius.

"Also dead," replied the general, "by his own hand. He locked himself inside his house and opened his veins in the bath. I have set a guard on the house, and will have him decently buried once all is calm again."

Pastor and Asclepiodotus were the last casualties of the siege. The eight hundred Goths holed up inside the palace had little food and water to sustain them, and soon came to terms. Incredibly, Belisarius persuaded them to turn their coats and enlist under our standards. No further proof is needed of the mercenary nature of the Roman army at this time, and I found myself marching alongside the same Gothic axe-men that would gladly have chopped me in two during the struggle on the walls.

Belisarius set the surviving citizens to clean up the debris. He blamed them, not the Goths, for the ruin of Naples. They had failed to heed his warnings, mocked his offers of clemency, and thus brought misery and destruction on themselves.

I felt some degree of guilt for the sack, but it soon passed. This was war, and I had seen and suffered too much to fall prey to sentiment.

"Now our mission begins in earnest," said Procopius on the eve of our departure.

His lugubrious features glowed with something like holy zeal. "Forget Sicily and Naples. These were mere distractions from our true object. The Eternal City, Coel. Rome! She has been in the hands of barbarians for over a century, but Belisarius will reclaim her for the Empire."

I shared his enthusiasm. To me Rome was a mythical city like Troy or Olympus, an ideal rather than a place, spoken of in hushed whispers by the bards and storytellers of my youth. Now I would help to liberate the ancient birthplace of an empire that had conquered most of the known world.

It was something to boast of to my grandchildren, assuming I ever had any, and the prize seemed well within our grasp. The Roman army, when led by Belisarius, was invincible, and the Goths under Theodatus had proved a weak and indecisive enemy, incapable of bringing their greater numbers to bear.

Then, even as I sat and swilled wine with Procopius in a tavern that had somehow avoided being plundered, a breathless envoy arrived from the palace.

"General Belisarius demands to see you at once, sir," he panted, leaning against the doorframe.

"What is it?" snapped Procopius, shaking off the wine fumes and rising from his chair.

"A messenger just arrived by boat from the north. The Goths have deposed Theodatus and elected a new king in his stead. The new man is called Vitiges."

This name meant nothing to me then, but my hand still trembles to write it. In place of the weak and timid Theodatus, the Goths had chosen a humble officer of obscure origin but considerable ability and force of will. Like Stozes, Vitiges had a gift for unifying a defeated people, and stirring them to fresh defiance.

Procopius hurried to the palace to discuss this new threat with Belisarius and his generals. I stayed, finishing off my wine and sadly tracing another name in a puddle of stale liquid on the table.

Elene.

12.

In common with most deposed kings, Theodatus didn't last long. The Gothic nobles met at Regeta to pass his sentence of deposition and to proclaim the new king. As was their custom, they raised Vitiges on their shields, and his name was chanted by the assembled mass of soldiers.

Vitiges' coronation took place even as we marched from Naples and advanced on Rome. Reluctant to weaken his already slender forces, Belisarius left three hundred men to garrison Naples, and a similar number at the fortress of Cumae, the only other stronghold of note in Campania. These necessary losses were more than compensated by the eight hundred Goths he had enlisted at Naples, though like many of our foederati troops they were treacherous and fought only for money. It was one of the miracles of Belisarius' glorious career, that he achieved so much despite being almost always outnumbered, and with men who cared little for his causes.

Our army marched along the newer road, called the Latin Way, though for the sake of romance we might have used the broad pavement of the Appian Way, which followed the same route just a few miles to the west. Procopius was seized with a kind of ecstasy at being so close to this famous highway, and galloped off to survey it without waiting for Belisarius' permission.

"It is a wonder of the world!" he enthused on his return, "even after nine centuries of use, the pavement is unbroken, and the flagstones smooth and polished like glass. Oh, that I should live to tread the same path as the legions of old, as Caesar and Mark Antony and the heroes of the Republic!"

I was keen to see the Appian Way for myself, but Belisarius allowed his soldiers no time for sightseeing. He had to reach and seize Rome before the Goths rallied under their vigorous new king.

It was now the beginning of December, and the fair summer was a distant memory. We struggled along the icy roads, buffeted by cold winds and pelting rain that soaked man and beast to the bone. I remember glancing over my shoulder and being struck with fear at how puny and vulnerable our little army appeared, bogged down in winter rain and ice, more like a wandering band of fugitives than a mighty host bent on conquest.

Belisarius had hopes that the Roman senate, along with the nobles and Catholic clergy, headed by Pope Silverius, would not support the election of Vitiges, and welcome us into Rome without a fight. Vitiges, like his predecessor, held to the Arian heresy, and was no friend to the Catholic faith.

His other great hope was that the deposed king, Theodatus, would escape and raise an army to reclaim his throne, thus splitting the Gothic nation. While the two factions tore each other apart, Belisarius could quietly take possession of the Eternal City. Then, after the Goths had all but destroyed each other, he would march out and sweep the survivors into the sea. Italy would be free of barbarians, and the heartlands of the Empire restored to her rightful rulers.

It was a good plan, but ruined by the prudence of Vitiges. After hearing news of the revolt against him, Theodatus had fled Rome and headed alone towards Ravenna, hoping to raise support there. Vitiges sent an officer after him, a young man who apparently held some private grudge against Theodatus. The officer pursued the fugitive night and day and eventually overtook him at the fifth milestone from Ravenna. There, Theodatus went down on his aged knees and begged for mercy, but the youth had none, and murdered him on the spot.

Word of Theodatus's death reached Belisarius at Albano, where he had made camp before making the final advance on Rome, just a few miles to the north-east. He camped near the crumbling remains of the Castra Albana, a series of military camps built by some long-dead Emperor to station his legions near Rome. A flourishing town had sprung up the ruins, but the inhabitants locked and barred their gates against us.

I was desperate to clap eyes on Rome, but Belisarius remained in camp for a full day and night, waiting for a response to the latest message he had sent to Pope Silverius and the senators.

Once again the campaign hovered on the edge of catastrophe. If the Romans followed the example of the Neopolitans, and held true to their Gothic conquerors, we would be faced with the task of reducing the strongest city in Italy.

Vitiges had withdrawn to Ravenna, where dire rumours reached us of the enormous host he was collecting from all corners of the Gothic nation. Unknown to us at the time, he was also in talks with the three Kings of the Franks who had previously sworn a pact with Justinian. In return for various bribes and promises, they agreed to betray the Emperor, and secretly send as many troops as they could spare to aid Vitiges.

"There are no clever stratagems that will fool the Romans," said Procopius, "Belisarius has used up his supply of tricks and good fortune. There are four thousand Goths inside Rome, and over a hundred and fifty thousand of the brutes mustering at Ravenna and other places."

"A hundred and fifty thousand?" I scoffed, "that is an absurd figure. The entire Vandal nation in arms at Tricamarum was no more than fifty thousand. No people on earth can muster that many warriors."

He gave a mournful little shake of his head. "You forget, Coel, I have agents and spies planted all over the country. The Goths and Ostrogoths and their foul kinsmen are as numerous as locusts. If Vitiges draws all his power together, Belisarius cannot hope to face him in the field. Our pathetic little army would be crushed underfoot. Our only hope is to take Rome, strengthen its walls and endure the worst that the Goths can throw at us."

"To what end? Even if we take the city, how long can we possibly hold it against such a monstrous host? Does Belisarius hope for reinforcements from the Emperor?"

"Yes. Justinian envies his golden general, and is far too willing to listen to liars and flatterers who would have him believe that Belisarius is a traitor, but he cannot simply abandon us to our fate."

He held up a narrow finger. "One defeat, Coel. The Roman Empire stands perpetually on the edge of oblivion. One defeat is all it would take to tip us over the edge. Justinian cannot afford to throw away twelve thousand men."

"I remember Narses saying something to that effect," I said, "on the dockside at Constantinople, as we watched the fleet assemble for the expedition to North Africa. There was a time when Rome could muster ten legions for a campaign."

"Precisely. Now we can barely scrape together as many as three, and most of our troops are barbarians and sell-swords. We are living in the latter days, Coel. All is vanity."

I looked at him in surprise. Belisarius had used those very words to me, in the garden at Carthage, and the defeated Vandal king, Gelimer, had wailed them as he was paraded through the streets in Constantinople. Then I remembered that Procopius was closer to the general than I, and must have picked up the saying from him.

Our pessimistic mood lasted until an envoy finally arrived from Rome. He brought the news we longed for. Pope and Senate had decided to resist the Goths, and welcome the arrival of Belisarius with open arms.

Belisarius was on his feet and barking orders almost before the envoy had finished speaking. Infused with his spirit, our army shook itself into life and prepared to advance the last few miles to Rome.

Even as our soldiers broke camp, Belisarius turned from a meeting of his captains and beckoned at me.

"I must apologise," he said, offering me his hand, "I meant to speak with you after the capture of Naples, but lacked the opportunity. Procopius told me you were the man who explored the aqueduct and discovered the secret way into the city. Yet another fine service you have performed, for which Rome thanks you."

He vigorously shook my hand. I reddened, but he waved away the modest protests forming on my lips. "There is something else. Words are not enough. You are far too capable and useful a man to languish in my Guards, watching over my tent at night. I will give you a commission, and make you a captain of horse."

It sounded very fine, but in reality he made me a decanus, that is, a low-ranking officer in charge of ten cavalrymen. He was far too canny a soldier to place a man with no experience of command in charge of anything greater. The next rank up was centenarius, commanding a hundred men, which would have put me in a position to do some serious harm to our own side if I proved incompetent.

Still, it was another mark of favour, and another slap in the face of those who wished me ill. I never knew what was said between Belisarius and Procopius in private, but suspect that Procopius may have suggested that I needed a permanent bodyguard of my own. Belisarius knew I had enemies, though he was still blind to the deceits and intrigues of his wife.

"Thank you, sir," I replied, bowing my head. I glanced sideways and spotted Photius standing among a little knot of officers. Our eyes met for the first time since our brief combat at Membresa. I gave the hilt of Caledfwlch a meaningful pat. The message was clear: your time will come.

The men he gave me were of the race of the Heruli, the tribe of Germanic foederati troops I had lived and trained with for a time outside Constantinople. Belisarius knew my history, so it was probably a deliberate choice.

I had picked up some of their language, and my wrists and arms still bore the faded blue tattoo-marks inked onto them by Girenas, one of the few close friends I made among that clannish people. Poor Girenas had succumbed to the disease that swept through our fleet on the voyage to north Africa, but the marks were enough to overcome the initial suspicion and reticence of the men in my new command. They were good soldiers, disciplined after their fashion, with decent gear and horses, and lacking an officer since their previous decanus was killed during the street-fighting in Naples.

My men were attached to a cohort commanded by Bessas, and so now I was one of his subordinates instead of the ambivalent position I had held as a member of Belisarius' personal guard.

"Some men might regard this as a demotion," he said, grinning at me, "swapping the easy life of a glorified bodyguard to serve as a junior officer of horse? You will have no easy time of it, I assure you."

"I have no desire for an easy life, sir," I replied stoutly, and remembered to salute. He sneered at me and moved on, roaring at his captains to get their troops into line. I knew Bessas as a brave and capable officer, if bloodthirsty, and trusted by Belisarius. In later years I would discover another, much darker, side to his character.

Our army advanced on Rome, and I shall never forget the moment we descended the ridge of Albano, and the Eternal City lay spread out before us.

She was not quite as magnificent as I had pictured her, shimmering like some dream-city in a deathless summer haze. This was winter, and the city of stone and marble that lay before us was suited to the season. My overriding image is of a great expanse of stark grey and white buildings, with the gaunt silhouettes of the Circus Maximus and Capitol Hill looming over all.

The fading images of my childhood are dominated by my first clear sight of Constantinople, the mother of cities and apex of the world, straddling the Bosphorus like a vast glittering jewel. By comparison Rome was less grand, less opulent and exotic, and yet had a stern, forbidding majesty all of her own.

We advanced towards the city from the south, towards the Asinarian gate. Joy of joys, the gates stood open, and a great cheer rolled down the length of our army as the word spread: Rome had submitted, and the object of our conquest was achieved without a blow being struck.

Bessas' cohort formed part of the vanguard, and Belisarius ordered us forward to secure the gate. As we rode closer, a man became visible standing alone under the arch.

He was a Goth of noble status, his long fair hair brushed and powdered until it floated about his shoulders, clad in shining silver mail and a red woolen cloak fringed with white fur. An empty scabbard of red leather hung from his belt, and at his feet lay a fine spatha with a jeweled hilt. Lying beside the sword was a ring carrying a number of large iron keys.

Bessas summoned me to his side. "Your first duty," he said, "go and speak to that idiot and find out who he is."

I spurred forward, conscious of the eyes of the entire army on me, and raised my empty right hand in greeting, to show that I meant no harm.

"Welcome home, Roman," said the Goth, folding his massive arms, "you have been too long away."

He was a fine-looking man, blue-eyed and handsome in a ruddy sort of way. I smiled at his mistake.

"I am a Briton in the service of Rome," I replied, reining in, "and my home lies many thousands of miles from here. As does yours. Why do you stand under the gate?"

"To yield up the city. My name is Leuderis, commander of the garrison of Rome. Or I was until my men chose to abandon their posts. They marched out via the Flaminian gate, and even now are fleeing north, like whipped dogs, to seek Vitiges."

I rested my fist on my hip. "But you stayed?"

"Yes. I stayed. Your General Belisarius is free to take me prisoner, or hang me, or whatever he sees fit."

"There lies my sword," he added, nodding at the blade, "and the keys of Rome. You may tell Belisarius that the city is his."

13.

On the tenth day of December, Belisarius entered the Eternal City and reclaimed it for the Empire. He did so informally, wasting no time on formal processions or grand proclamations, though he did have the royal Gothic banners on Capitol Hill torn down and replaced with our imperial standards. For the first time in over a hundred years, the purple and gold flew over Rome.

He treated Leuderis with honour, and sent him back to Constantinople as a captive, along with the keys to the city. Then he immediately set about the work of putting Rome in a state of defence. The city had flourished again under the rule of Theoderic the Great and his successors, but the walls had been allowed to fall into ruin, and needed to be repaired before the arrival of Vitiges and his hordes of Gothic warriors.

The bewildered citizens, who had lined the streets to welcome our soldiers, found themselves ignored, save those Belisarius hired as extra labour. He met with the Pope and the Senate, of course, and treated them with all due honour and courtesy, but diplomacy was never Belisarius' greatest strength. They were a pack of treacherous swine, good for nothing save plotting in darkened corners, and began scheming against Belisarius almost as soon as he marched into the city.

For days all was intense bustle and activity, and I found myself obliged to pick up a shovel and play the role of workman. Rome's ancient, decaying ramparts were bolstered and strengthened, bastions and towers constructed, fresh battlements erected to replace those that had collapsed and fallen away, great holes in the walls plugged with fresh masonry, or earth and timber if stone was lacking. The defensive ditch that surrounded the city had been completely neglected, choked with weeds and rubbish, and had to be cleared, deepened and extended. Meanwhile our fleet transported fresh supplies of corn from Sicily, which were stored inside Rome's many granaries, so we would not starve during the inevitable siege.

I had imagined that the Romans would be delighted to see the powerful fortifications rising around them, and rush to our aid. It soon became clear they had surrendered the city, not out of patriotic reasons, but as an act of craven self-preservation.

"Why do you waste your strength, throwing up these walls?" I remember one stout citizen yelling at me as I rested on my spade, "Rome is too large for you to defend her at every point, and the Goths too numerous! You must fly, fly back to the east, before you are surrounded and destroyed!"

I rubbed the back of my hand across my face, wiping away some of the sweat and grime, and sighed. "We have only just arrived," I said patiently, "are you tired of our presence already?"

His eyes bulged, veins constricting on his broad forehead, and he waved his arms at me. "You mock!" he shouted, "let us see how you laugh when the Goths spread your naked body on the blood-eagle and split your ribs open!"

This was the first I had heard of the Goths indulging in this particularly gruesome form of execution, said to be practiced by the wild tribes of the Scotti in the furthest northern reaches of Britain.

"You must be a learned man," I remarked, picking up my shovel, "or else prey to a fevered imagination. Now I must go on with my work." He continued to rave at me, and my comrades, as we piled up a great heap of earth and stones to form a rampart near one of the city's northern gates, close to the Mausoleum of Augustus. I was fascinated by this enormous circular tomb, built by the first Emperor to house the earthly remains of the imperial family, but as yet had enjoyed no leisure to study it. Belisarius kept his soldiers hard at work, and none worked harder than the men of Bessas' cohort.

Procopius, of course, crawled all over the ancient ruins and monuments like an endlessly inquisitive ant, gasping and exclaiming at each new find. I rarely spoke to him now, thanks to my new duties, but he occasionally sought me out to enthuse about the wonders of Rome and its history. I believe Belisarius ordered him to check on me, out of concern for Caledfwlch.

"That sword is a sacred trust," Procopius would often say, "personally I would have wrenched it from your grasp long ago, and sent it for safe-keeping in Constantinople. It should be gathering dust among the other heirlooms of Empire, safely guarded in the deepest vault of the Great Palace."

"You are welcome to try and take it from me," I said with a slight edge of warning in my voice, "Calcdfwlch never leaves my sight. This sword is my constant companion. The only true and lasting friend I have ever known."

He sniffed. "I am not in the least bit surprised. You are a surly brute, entirely devoid of manners and graces, and it is like you to make friends with a bit of metal."

While we laboured and sweated to turn Rome back into the impregnable fortress she had once been, storm-clouds were gathering in the north of Italy. Vitiges had mustered his great host near Ravenna, every bit as strong and numerous as Procopius feared, and began his march on Rome.

The ground must have quaked under the tread of so many men. I quaked in my camp-bed at night, picturing hordes of barbarians converging on the city, long lines of gleaming spears and black banners.

The folly and arrogance of Justinian were thrown into stark relief. Our proud, ambitious little Caesar had sent us all to our deaths, while he sat in his splendid palace at Constantinople, safe and comfortable and surrounded by every conceivable luxury.

At his side sat Theodora, that evil woman, as spiteful as she was beautiful, who had done her best to murder me. Her painted face faded from my mind, replaced by the ugly features of Narses, the dwarfish eunuch who had tried to break me and make me his agent. Was he behind the recent attempts on my life, or were Antonina and Photius still the Empress's creatures? Who did Elene serve, and would I ever see her again?

I will see you again, before you die…

Those were her last words to me, at the ruins of the aqueduct outside Naples. It was the height of folly to suppose that she had meant them with affection. Any love that existed between us was dead, destroyed, like everything else good in my life, by the cruelty of my enemies.

Everything except Caledfwlch. Try as they might, they could not take the sword from me. I hugged the blade at night, and in the small hours fancied that I could hear the voices of the trapped souls inside, whispering to me.

Belisarius had no intention of sitting and waiting inside the city for the Goths to come to him. Despite his slender resources and numbers, he dispatched troops to conquer the surrounding countryside and capture towns and fortresses, hoping the presence of so many Roman garrisons would impede the Gothic advance.

The region of Samnium submitted to us, and the city of Benevento opened its gates. Procopius visited Benevento, and was transported to new heights of ecstasy when he discovered the gigantic tusks of an ancient boar, some twenty-seven inches long and still sharp as a dagger. According to local legend, it had taken thirty warriors to bring down this demonic pig, which reminded of similar tales of the Twrch Trwyth in Britain.

Bessas was sent out with some light horse to capture the hilltop town of Narni, strategically important as it occupied a key position on the Via Flamini, the road that connected Rome to the Adriatic Sea.

I and my little troop were part of Bessas' company, no more than two hundred strong, that rode out north of the Flaminian gate. The town itself was a pretty place, overhanging a narrow gorge over a river, and might have proved difficult to take had the citizens not yielded it up without a fight.

"God grant that Vitiges comes soon," Bessas grumbled, "I have not smelled blood since Naples. These people are too easily conquered."

We were soon to enjoy a surfeit of blood. In February another detachment of cavalry was sent out, this time commanded by Constantine – the grateful officer Procopius and I had rescued from the stake at Membresa – with some of Bessas' troops in support.

Constantine's orders were to enter Tuscany and take the towns of Spoleto and Perugia. Again, the Italian citizens surrendered both places readily enough, and hailed us as friends rather than conquerors.

Perugia was some fifty miles north of Rome, and directly on the Gothic line of march from Ravenna. Constantine was over-confident, and neglected to post scouts while he secured the town and chose men to leave behind as a garrison.

A spearman patrolling the northern wall was the first to see them. "Horsemen to the north!" I heard him shout, his voice tinged with panic.

I ran up the steps onto the walkway, followed by my men, and leaned over the wall to look north, where the sentry pointed his spear.

There was a considerable haze of dust approaching from that direction, steadily growing larger as it rolled across the network of fields and woods outside the town, silhouetted against a backdrop of dreaming hills.

The dust cleared a little, and I made out a troop of horsemen, eighty or so, riding in skirmish formation.

"Nothing to worry about," I muttered, willing it to be true, "probably a scouting party, miles ahead of Vitiges' main army."

"You are wrong, sir," said one of my men – the Heruli are a miserable lot, and insolent with it – "look there. More riders."

I could have cursed him, but he was right. My eighty horse-archers swiftly became a hundred, and then two hundred, and behind them sixty or so heavy cavalry, in scale mail and helmets with streaming horse-tail plumes, carrying large round shields and spathas as well as their long spears. This was surely no band of scouts, but part of the Gothic vanguard. The rest of their massive host could not be far behind.

We might have stayed behind the walls of Perugia and left the Goths to ride around uselessly outside, for they had no infantry or siege equipment.

"Vitiges will not waste time laying siege to Perugia," I said confidently, "he will bypass us and march on to Rome."

Constantine, however, was not one for skulking behind walls. Trumpets sounded through the streets, summoning us to arms. Forcing down my excitement, I led my men to the stables where we had left our horses. We mounted and rode back to the northern gates.

Our commander was already drawing up his men on the fields outside. He was an excitable figure, splendid as any Roman general in his polished armour, riding up and down in front of our line and howling at our men to get into position.

We numbered almost three hundred riders, a few more than the Goths, and like them a mixture of horse-archers and mailed lancers. I led my men to join the rest of Bessas' soldiers on the left wing, a hundred or so Huns and Heruls.

Our little army was drawn up in three divisions. I glanced north, and my mouth dried up as I observed the Goths forming up for battle. Their own lancers were in the centre, with horse-archers spread out wide to right and left. A few of the braver souls rode forward to taunt us, shaking their spears and yelling insults.

"Soldiers of Rome!" Constantine shouted, his face scarlet with the effort of shouting, "fear not these barbarians! Put your faith in God, cast your javelins at them, bring them down with your lances, and you shall have victory!"

I had heard Belisarius make similar speeches on the eve of battle, and it was obvious that Constantine was consciously aping the general, even down to his splendid armour and style of oratory. Now he wanted to take his hero-worship and mimicry a step further, and win a great victory on the battlefield.

To speak plain, Constantine had chosen to endanger his men simply to gratify his ego. He drew his sword with a flourish and shouted the order to attack.

His tactics were unsubtle: straight at the Goths, hit them between the eyes – between the legs, as Bessas later described it with one of his feral grins – and scatter them to the four winds.

Our left wing surged forward, with me and my ten Heruls in the front rank on the extreme left. To my right, our Hunnish lancers whooped and shrieked like the savages they were, urging their heavy horses into a gallop. Constantine galloped ahead of them, bent low over his beast's neck.

We spread out as we charged, to match the loose formation of the Gothic horse-archers. Half their number had peeled away to avoid contact and shoot into our flanks, while the rest spurred forward to engage us head-on.

The most difficult skill a horse-soldier can learn is the art of shooting a bow from the saddle while controlling the horse with his knees. I had spent hundreds of hours in the camp of the Heruli trying to master it, with limited success.

This was real combat, not a drill-yard, so instead I plucked one of the two light javelins hanging from my saddle and drew it to my shoulder, aiming at the contorted face of the Goth streaking towards me.

He had put aside his bow and drawn a thin, curved sword. I let fly with my javelin. He wrenched his pony aside in time to avoid it, and the missile plunged harmlessly to his left. I had time to draw Caledfwlch before we closed, and then it was blade to blade as both sides surged together.

All was chaos and noise and terror, horses shrieking, men shouting, steel clashing. I parried the Goth's wild lunge, stabbed at his face, missed, punched him with the grip of Caledfwlch, yelled in pain as I bruised my knuckles on his bony jaw. It was enough to unseat him, and he fell away, vanishing among the conflicting waves of riders.

A red-bearded face flashed before me. I drove the point of my sword at it and felt my wrist shudder with the impact. Blood spattered up my arm. I felt a surge of exultation – got one! – and looked around for my men. They were close behind me, spearing Goths with controlled fury and lethal efficiency.

"On them!" I shouted, though they hardly needed telling, "cut them to pieces!"

The rest of the fight is a blur. I killed another Goth, I think, and suffered a minor wound on the shoulder, but events are often compressed in my memory. Now it seems to me that only seconds passed before the Goths broke and fled. Constantine's headlong charge had taken them by surprise, and our lancers were more numerous and superior to theirs.

My men were eager to pursue the beaten enemy, but I held them back, not wishing to lose them among that great mass of men and horses retreating towards the hills. Constantine also kept a tight rein on his troops. His trumpeters sounded the recall, summoning back those of our men who hared after the Goths, while his silver-armoured figure rode back and forth, triumphant, over-excited, the light of victory shining in his eyes.

He spotted me, biting back curses as one of my soldiers wrapped a bandage round the cut on my shoulder, and galloped over.

"Coel!" he shouted, holding aloft his bloody sword, "my friend and saviour, it is good to see you! What a fight, eh? Look at them run! Have you taken a nick, then?"

"It is nothing," I said with forced modesty, and truly it was not, a shallow gash from a Gothic spear, but I have never been very good at enduring pain.

He glanced at it with fleeting concern, and then his mind flitted back to higher matters. "Look at that!" he exclaimed, indicating the battlefield, "how many Goths did we kill, do you think? A hundred, at least!

I did a quick head-count. Certainly there were more Goths stretched out on the field than Romans, but unlike them we could ill-afford the casualties. I was tempted to say so, but it seemed a shame to spoil Constantine's little victory.

My fears that the Gothic war-band we had driven off was merely part of Vitiges' advance guard proved groundless. The King of the Goths was still at Ravenna, but news of the defeat outside Perugua seems to have spurred him into action.

He divided his enormous host, sending part of it into Dalmatia. In an attempt to distract the Goths, Justinian had ordered the remains of Mundus's troops in Illyria to cross the border and do as much damage as they could before withdrawing again.

Vitiges then led the rest of his army, which still numbered some one hundred and fifty thousand men, south towards Rome. Belisarius hurriedly recalled Bessas and Constantine, instructing them to leave small garrisons in the towns we had captured.

Bessas, who unwisely despised the Goths and rated them poor soldiers, was slow in retreating, and almost caught by the vanguard of the Gothic host. He managed to extricate himself, not without heavy loss, and led the survivors of his command in an undignified scramble back to Rome.

I was ordered to accompany the main part of Constantine's force back to the city. The Goths pressed hard on our heels as we rode at a hard gallop along the Via Flaminia, the ancient road leading to the Flaminian Gate. Constantine called a halt when we reached the Milvian Bridge, two miles north of Rome.

This great stone causeway over the Tiber had been the scene of an epic battle between the Emperor Constantine and his rival Maxentius, some two hundred years previously. Constantine won, and went on to move the capital of the empire from Rome to a decrepit fishing port on the Bosphorus, which he modestly named after himself.

The bridge was the main route to Rome, and the Goths would have to cross it. Knowing this, Belisarius built an enormous wooden tower on the southern side of the river, six levels high and with fighting platforms for archers to rain missiles down on anyone advancing over the bridge. The tower commanded the passage over the river, and was manned with a strong garrison of Isaurians.

Constantine hailed the soldiers in the tower as we rested our horses on the northern side before crossing.

"There is a fine difference between an orderly withdrawal and headlong flight," he said, "I don't want the barbarians to think we are running away."

Running away was precisely what we were doing, but again I didn't want to shatter his delusions.

I shaded my eyes to look north. As expected, I glimpsed a great storm of dust rolling across the plains, and felt the earth tremble slightly underfoot, like a distant earthquake.

"They are coming," one of my soldiers said bleakly.

I swallowed. They were coming. A hundred and fifty thousand Goths, hot for revenge against the pathetic handful of Romans that had dared to invade their land.

The siege of Rome had begun.

14.

The Goths came on fast, ignoring our garrisons at Narni and Spoleto and Perugua. Vitiges was not to be distracted from the main prize, and all of the obstacles Belisarius had strewn in his path failed to impede his advance for a second. All, save the tower guarding the Milvian Bridge.

Our soldiers, including myself, crowded the walls beside the Flaminian Gate to watch the innumerable squadrons of the Gothic vanguard march into view.

Like locusts, Procopius had described the Gothic host, and it seemed an apt description. A horrified silence fell over our men as the enemy spread across the land north of the bridge.

One hundred and fifty thousand men. It sounds meaningless, a mere statistic, until you see them in the flesh. It was as though Hell had vomited up its legions of the damned, rank after rank, squadron after squadron of barbarians.

I still call them barbarians, an arrogant conceit I picked up from the Romans, but they were no undisciplined horde of savages. They had learned the art of war from Rome, and deployed with a smooth, calm efficiency that would have brought a happy tear to the eye of Agricola or Scipio Africanus.

"Vitiges is in no hurry," remarked Procopius, who stood to my left, "he likes to sup his vengeance cold, this one. Pity. I had hoped he would charge at Rome like a bull, and dash his brains out against our defences."

"We are dead men," a soldier muttered to my right, "how can we resist such a multitude? Belisarius has brought us to our deaths."

"Stop whimpering," I said angrily, "the Goths have not won a single victory against us. Every time we fight them, they surrender or run away screaming, like frightened children."

He smiled bitterly. "I would think twice before facing a hundred and fifty thousand children, sir."

"A hundred and fifty thousand, or half a million, it makes no odds," I said dismissively, "they cannot cross the bridge. Let them sit on the northern banks of the Tiber and shout insults at us. They will soon grow hoarse with shouting, and turn for home."

Brave words, uttered with conviction, but it was all an act. I knew the Goths were not children, and that the tower over the Milvian Bridge could not hold them forever, but I was trying to play the role of an officer and raise morale. Judging from the cynical expressions of the soldiers who heard me, I had overplayed it.

Belisarius intended the tower to delay the Gothic advance, obliging them to waste valuable time building boats or marching around to find some other bridge. Such an enormous host could only be kept in the field with difficulty, and would eventually start to break up. Once that happened, Belisarius could ride out and destroy the scattered Gothic armies in turn.

Such was my understanding of his strategy. The morning after our return to Rome, he led out a thousand of his men to camp on the shores of the Tiber and observe the movements of the enemy. He took Bessas with him, which meant my little command was part of the expedition.

Had I know what would follow, I might have feigned illness or injury, anything to keep me safe inside the walls of Rome.

It was a sharp morning in the dying days of winter, cold and with a smattering of frost on the ground, but with the scent of spring and renewal in the air. Some of the pessimism among our men had died away, for the Goths had not moved overnight, and the dark mass of their army was still encamped beyond the northern side of the bridge.

Belisarius wore his golden armour, as though on parade, and rode his famous white-faced bay. I remember being cheered by the sight of him riding at the head of the column, our peerless general, with the purple and gold imperial standard fluttering above his head.

We spread out in a double line and approached the bridge at an easy canter. The Goths had no catapults or ballistae set up on the northern side of the bridge, and we were well out of bowshot. I imagined Belisarius standing on the southern banks of the Tiber and thumbing his nose at the enemy, and smiled.

Half a mile from the bridge, our trumpeters sounded the halt. We reined in with practiced discipline, and Belisarius trotted forward a few steps, leaning forward in the saddle to study the tower.

Suddenly he wheeled his bay in a circle and galloped back to our line. "Back!" I heard him shout, his voice hoarse and urgent, "back to the city, at once!"

More trumpets sounded, not ours, but from the north. Hundreds of Gothic cavalry were pouring over the bridge. For a terrible moment I thought the tower had been abandoned, but then I saw helmets gleaming on the upper levels. I waited, expecting our Isaurians to unleash a deadly hail of arrows.

Nothing happened. Even as our trumpets squealed the retreat, and I barked at my men to turn about, the full horror of the situation dashed over me like freezing water.

The men in the tower were Goths. Somehow they had seized it during the night, slaughtering or driving away the garrison. That was impossible. Our sentries on the Flaminian Gate kept a constant vigil on the tower. If the Goths had attempted an assault, the Isaurians would have sounded the alarm. Belisarius kept a strong body of Hunnish lancers on permanent alert, ready to ride out and aid the garrison.

The Goths moved fast, determined to catch Belisarius in the open before he reached the safety of the city. We fled back across the plain with the taste of fear in our mouths. I lashed my horse's flanks with my spurs until the poor animal bled, growling at her to find an extra burst of speed.

Belisarius reached the Flaminian Gate and shouted at the soldiers on the ramparts to admit us. They hesitated.

"What ails you?" he screamed, snatching off his helmet, "why do you delay? See, it is me, your general! Open the gates!"

They refused to obey. Terrified by the sudden onset of the Goths, the men on the rampart abandoned all notions of duty and courage, and thought only of their own safety.

Belisarius cursed and railed at them, threatening all kinds of dire punishments, to no avail. They vanished, and we were left stranded outside the city with thousands of baying Goths closing in behind us.

A lesser man might have lost his head completely. Belisarius wheeled around, his face ashen, and addressed his officers.

"You, sirs! Why are you standing there like a pack of lost sheep? Bessas, your cohort will form the left flank. Constantine, the right. I will lead my guards in the centre. Move!"

He was going to attack. It seemed insane, but what else could we do, save wait to be slaughtered?

I barely had time to think. Bessas roared us into line, forming up in a single column on the left, while Belisarius arranged his guards. My horse neighed and tossed her head, and I soothed her with a trembling hand, gulping and breathing fast as I observed the approach of the Goths.

Some two to three thousand had crossed by now, and were thundering towards us in a wild, all-out charge. Their red and black banners streamed in the wind, while the sound of their deep-throated war-yells rolled like thunder across the plain.

To oppose that rapidly advancing horror was to embrace death. Another few seconds, and I might have shied away, my courage stretched and snapped beyond endurance, but the sound of the trumpets called me to my duty.

"Charge, charge, charge!" howled Bessas, kicking his own bay into life. His cohort surged after him, straight at the solid wall of iron and horseflesh flowing towards us.

Then I heard it, another cry leaping from thousands of Gothic throats and rippling around the field like a forest fire:

That is Belisarius! Kill the bay! Kill the bay!

Our general's fame had worked against him. His golden armour and white-faced bay were famous across the known world, and he made no attempt to hide himself, galloping at the head of his guards, his lance aimed at the heart of the Gothic line.

Then we were among them. I found myself guarding against two Goths at once, taking their blows on my shield. The half-healed cut on my right shoulder burst. Warm blood flowed down my arm as I struggled to hold my beaten and dented shield upright.

One of the Goths was young, with just a frizz of blonde hair on his chin and upper lip, and too eager. I leaned back in the saddle, his spatha slashed inches past my face, and darted forward to stab at his throat. Caledfwlch's blade slid easily in and out of his flesh, and he jerked and tumbled away, blood gushing down his breastplate.

The second Goth tried to beat me down with sheer strength. He almost succeeded. Chips flew from the ragged edges of my shield as his sword scraped and banged against it. I let him blow himself out, and then gave him the point, missing his eye but smashing in several of his teeth.

"Guard the general! Guard the general!"

Bessas' voice, rising above the clash of weapons and the wild howls of the Goths. A gap appeared to my right among the waves of horsemen. I briefly glimpsed Belisarius, locked in a duel with an enormous Gothic chieftain over twice his size.

The combat seemed unequal, but Belisarius' sword was the quicker, and whipped out the chieftain's throat. His opponent had no sooner fallen than his Guards clustered around him, raising and interlocking their shields to form an impenetrable wall around their master.

Bessas had led his troop to join the wall, and was bawling at the rest of his command to fall in line. Belisarius had to be protected. If he fell, our cause was lost.

I shouted at my men to obey. We attached ourselves to the left flank, and more men flowed in behind us, until a ring of wood and metal was presented to the Goths. I gritted my teeth, gasping at the pain of my re-opened wound and the impact of spears and javelins thudding against my tattered shield.

After a time the Goths gave back, and it was safe to lower my shield and take stock. They were retreating towards the river, leaving a great number of dead and wounded scattered across the plain.

Constantine had charged to the rescue, hitting them in flank and rolling them up while they tried to break our line. I saw Belisarius, untouched despite the best efforts of the enemy, raise his sword and order another charge.

"Drive them to the river!" he shouted, "drown these beasts in the Tiber, and give their souls to Hades!"

I was sweating, bleeding, panic-struck, my heart threatening to burst out of my chest. Another charge into this inexhaustible horde of devils was beyond me, but we did it, spurring forward and pursuing the fugitives, coming up with them even as they tried to re-form on the banks of the river.

I washed Caledfwlch in Gothic blood, until I was red to the shoulders and could barely see for a film of sweat and dirt and gore. We butchered them like pigs, but still more stormed across the Milvian Bridge, including a squadron of spearmen on foot, many thousands strong.

A good part of our command was scattered or slain, and we had no hope of resisting the Gothic infantry. Their ring-mail shined like mirrors in the cold winter sun, and the sight of their long-axes sent a shudder through me, awakening bad memories of the desperate fight for the walls at Naples.

Belisarius signaled the retreat, but the Flaminian Gate was still closed against us. In desperation, he led us onto a rising patch of ground, about midway between the river and the city. There he arranged us into a sort of human fortress, with half our remaining soldiers dismounted and forming a hollow circle of shields, while the remainder waited inside, resting their horses and preparing to sally forth when Belisarius gave the order.

A third of my men were dead, and the survivors every bit as bloody and exhausted as their chief. I stood, leaning on a borrowed spear for support, blinking away blood and sweat from my eyes as fresh waves of Goths charged towards our miserably slender battle-line.

Kill Belisarius! Kill Belisarius!

"What about the rest of us, you bastards!" I shouted back, a moment of grim humour in the face of disaster. I am still rather proud of it, considering death was about to stretch out his bony hand and snuff out my candle.

It was then I witnessed the noblest and most heroic act of the war. A young officer named Valentinian – I learned later that he was a great friend of Photius – suddenly broke out of our line and galloped straight at the advancing spears.

His mare foundered, unwilling to hurl herself on the points, but he vaulted from the saddle and vanished among the throng.

The disciplined, stately Gothic advance stumbled to a halt as men in the forward ranks turned to strike at Valentinian, who had leaped to his feet. He struck left and right with his sword, mowing down Goths like ripe corn, careless of the forest of spears that stabbed and thrust at him.

At last, slathered in blood, Valentinian fell, and was run through as he lay squirming on the ground. His sacrifice had a great effect on the Goths, who ignored the shouts of their captains and failed to resume their advance.

Perhaps they eyed us nervously, thinking that we were all like Valentinian, ready to fight to our last breath in defence of Rome. Thank God they could not see into my heart. I was spent, all used up, shaking with terror and fatigue, ready to lie down and welcome eternity. Another Gothic assault would have rolled over my head.

Belisarius acted before the spell cast by Valentinian's sacrifice broke. "Withdraw," I heard him say. His trumpeter sounded the weary note, and we began our retreat back to the city. The men on foot resumed their horses from the cavalry in the middle, and formed a rearguard as we retreated in good order.

The Goths stood and watched us go, like thousands of statues arranged in long lines. A strange hush fell over the field.

Our toils were not done, not yet. Twilight was sweeping in from the west, rendering everything dim and uncertain. As we passed beyond the ditch that lay outside the walls, a groan rippled down our line. The gates were still shut.

Drums started to beat behind us. The sound of doom. How long before the Goths recovered their courage?

"Soldiers," said Belisarius, addressing the sentinels on the Flaminian Gate, "for the love of God, open the gates. Do so, or bear my curse."

His voice sounded hollow and exhausted. Despite fighting in the front line for so many hours, he had not taken a single wound, but his golden armour was torn and dented, and liberally coated in blood. His helmet was gone, mangled in the fighting, and the light of the dying sun reflected from a sheen of perspiration on his balding scalp.

"We dare not, sir," replied one of the men on the gate, "if we open the gates, the Goths might force entry to the city."

Miserable coward! Black rage welled up inside me. I would have started forward and hurled obscenities at him, had others not already done so.

"Open those damned gates!" hollered Bessas, his bulky frame shaking with anger, "or I'll have the lot of you flayed alive and fed to the dogs!

Still the sentries prevaricated, and the sound I had dreaded reached my ears: the deep, drawn-out drone of a bull-horn. The Goths were advancing again.

"Constantine," Belisarius snapped, but the young officer had anticipated his orders and was already shouting at the battered remains of his squadron to form up.

Where they found the strength, God knows, but Constantine led them in one of his wild, fearless charges at the Gothic lancers advancing at a trot towards the city. Surprised, for they thought us spent, they were routed after a brief and vicious melee, and scattered back towards their own lines.

Constantine's men suffered severe losses, but this last success was enough to embolden the sentries on the rampart. Shame-faced, they at last opened the gates to admit us.

Weary and dispirited, weighed down by exhaustion and grieving at our losses, we led our plodding horses back into Rome. Night was falling, but there was no rest for Belisarius. Almost as soon as the gates were closed again, he ordered fires to be lit on the walls, to keep a watch through the night in case the Goths tried a sudden assault.

We had escaped, and preserved the life of our general, but there was no sense of victory. The Milvian Bridge had fallen, and now there was nothing to stop the Goths from crossing the Tiber and surrounding the city.

Our army was trapped, like rats in a cage.

15.

We scarcely had time to draw breath before a panicky rumour blew up that the Goths had broken into the city, overcoming our guards manning the gate of Saint Pancratius, on the Tuscan side of the Tiber.

"You must fly, sir," cried one of Belisarius' Guards, "there are secret ways in and out of Rome. Use them, and save yourself!"

Belisarius scowled at the man. "I have had my fill of cowards today," he said quietly, and called for Bessas.

"Take thirty men and investigate this alarm," he ordered. I quailed, praying that Bessas would not choose me. Thankfully, I and the remainder of my command were left behind. The rumour proved to be false anyway, spread by some of the more nervous citizens.

Once this final alarm had died down, Belisarius wearily took himself off to his quarters on the Capitol Hill, where his wife and her attendants waited to strip off his soiled armour, bathe his exhausted body and anoint his bruises with soft lotions and unguents.

I had access to no such luxuries, but had to be content with a quick wash in a water-butt, a mouthful of bread and wine, and a dreamless sleep on a hard pallet. I saw to my men first, or the six that remained. Four had spilled their life's blood on the field beyond the Flaminian Gate, though I did not see them die, and (to my shame) cannot recall their names or faces.

Next morning I woke feeling like an old man. My body was a mass of cramps and pains, and my wounded shoulder felt as though a fire had been lit inside my flesh.

Bessas allowed his officers little rest. I managed to swallow some coarse rye bread and a morsel of goat's cheese before the accursed trumpets were sounding again, summoning us to a briefing.

He had set up a table in a cobbled square, lined with shops and galleried walkways, and looked little the worse for wear as his surviving officers gathered around him.

"Brisk work yesterday," he snapped in his businesslike way, "I see some of you were hurt. Get used to it. The Goths have us sewn up."

I wondered at that. Rome was twelve miles in circumference, and even Vitiges' massive host would struggle to surround the entire city.

"They are building six main camps," he explained, "fortified in the usual way, ditches, stakes and earthen ramparts. As you know, or damn well should do, Rome has fourteen gates. Vitiges appears to be concentrating his infantry to cover seven of them. Five on the southern bank, two on the north. His cavalry is deploying to keep a watch on the remainder, so there is no escape."

Bessas flashed one of his crooked grins, as though there was something amusing about the situation.

"Regarding the tower on the Milvian Bridge," he went on, "some of you may be wondering how the Goths came to capture it. Well, earlier this morning a few Isaurian deserters came crawling back into the city, pleading for the general's forgiveness. They had been part of the garrison on the tower. Apparently they took fright at the size of the Gothic host and abandoned their posts during the night. The Goths forced the gates and seized the tower, just in time to ambush Belisarius when he sallied out of Rome."

"Will the general forgive them, sir?" asked one of my brother officers, "and the men on the Flaminian Gate who refused to admit us yesterday?"

"They should all die," commented another, to a general murmur of agreement, "flogged through the streets, and beheaded as traitors."

Bessas shrugged. "They will be punished, certainly, but not with death. We cannot afford to start reducing our own numbers with executions."

I disagreed. Mercy is a noble trait, but the presence of cowards and deserters within our ranks could only lower morale. My voice, however, was too faint to be heeded, so I kept quiet.

The Goths were soon firmly entrenched around the city, though as I suspected they lacked the numbers to encircle us completely. Their light horsemen scoured the countryside, but the passage between Rome and Campania was not completely cut off. If Justinian overcame his envious suspicions of Belisarius and saw fit to send enough reinforcements, they could still reach us from the south.

For the time being, we were stranded inside Rome, and could do nothing but watch helplessly as Vitiges took measures to starve us out. First he ordered his men to destroy the fourteen great aqueducts outside Rome, thinking to cut off our supply of water.

These ancient brick archways were duly dismantled, but the attempt to deprive us of water failed. The waters of the Tiber, though turgid, and the many wells located inside the city, were more than enough to supply our needs.

The destruction of the aqueducts did succeed in stemming the flow of water needed to turn the city mills. Without the mills, we could not grind corn for bread, and the supplies of Sicilian corn inside the granaries would soon be used up.

Belisarius devised a brilliant solution, proving he was something of an engineer as well as a soldier. He noticed that the current of the river flowed strongest under the Bridge of

Hadrian, which spanned the Tiber between the centre of Rome and Hadrian's mausoleum.

He consulted with his workmen, and they built facsimiles of the mills that no longer turned, small enough to be placed inside boats. The boats were then moored under the arches of the bridge, where the current of the river was powerful enough to turn them.

Ingenious, you might think, but the Goths soon got wind of this innovation, thanks to some deserters who fled the city at night and gave Vitiges the information in exchange for being allowed to pass unmolested. Our army was rotten with such traitors, and I often wondered if Belisarius was ever reduced to despair. If so, he did well to hide it in public, for he always appeared cheerful and lively, as though victory was just around the corner.

The Goths threw the rotting bodies of our soldiers, killed in the recent battle outside the walls, into the Tiber, along with tree trunks and various bits of rubbish. The strong current carried all this detritus down the Tiber, and it broke through the ropes guarding the bridge and smashed our boats all to pieces.

"What, have they sunk our mills?" Belisarius said lightly when he was informed of the disaster, "then we shall build new ones, and guard them with more care."

Undaunted, he ordered more of the floating mills to be constructed, and this time had several thick lengths of iron chain thrown across the outer side of the bridge. When the Goths threw more rubbish into the water, it got caught in the chains, giving our men on the banks time to fish it out with long hooks. Thus the mills continued to turn, and the city was adequately supplied with bread for weeks afterwards.

I saw little of Procopius, thanks to my new duties, until one day he appeared as me and my men were helping to block up the Flaminian Gate with piles of rubble. Belisarius had chosen to render the gate inaccessible, judging it too close to the Gothic lines and vulnerable to assault.

"Tacitus remarked that the Britons make poor workmen," I heard him say, "as lazy as they are rude and uncouth. I see now that his words had some merit."

I put down the heavy block I was carrying and slowly straightened up, wincing at the ache in my lower back. It was good to hear his voice, laden with its usual sarcasm.

"Romans are poorly placed to criticise the work of others," I said, turning, "since they never do any, but have to pay stronger races to do it for them."

Procopius was sitting on an upturned piece of masonry. He looked worn-out and thinner than ever, with dark smudges under his eyes. His hands, I noticed, were spotted with ink.

"You look well," he said, studying me with narrowed eyes, "save that bit of stained linen wrapped around your shoulder. Are you wounded?"

"Spear-cut," I replied, flexing the shoulder with a grimace, "it is healing, but still aches. Just a graze, really."

"Really. I've heard stronger men than you dismiss their wounds as nothing, and seen them buried a few days later. Let me look at it. I know something of medicine."

"You are a master of every art," I said sourly, but allowed him to gently unwrap the binding and poke his nose into the cut on my shoulder. It was scabbing over, but slower than I would have liked, and the pain was refusing to go away.

"No odour, thank God," he said, straightening, "but it needs washing out. Come with me."

I protested that I could not leave my duties, but Procopius' authority was second only to his master's, and the centenarian overseeing the work on the gate said nothing as he led me away.

He took me to the Pincian Hill, in the northeastern quarter of the city, where Belisarius had fixed his new headquarters. The hill offered an unrivalled view of the rest of the city, and the encampments of the Goths.

"The walls here are in a poor state," said Procopius, indicating the dilapidated and crumbling ramparts, "Belisarius has stationed himself here until they are repaired, to dissuade the Goths from trying an assault. He relies on the terror of his name to preserve Rome."

"Until when?" I said with asperity, "does he hope that Vitiges will simply give up and go away?"

"Something like that," replied Procopius, "at least the Gothic king is willing to talk."

Now I saw his real reason for bringing me here. A group of Gothic envoys were clustered at the foot of the steps leading up to the fine colonnaded mansion Belisarius had chosen for his headquarters.

The envoys were large, well-formed men, proud and arrogant in their bearing, clad in polished mail and fur-lined cloaks, their wrists and throats adorned with golden torcs. They clearly regarded themselves as superior beings, and disdained to look at the short, swarthy Isaurian spearmen who had escorted them into the city.

After a time they were admitted to the house, escorted by a strong guard. Procopius and I followed the procession up the steps, into a large, echoing hall of white marble.

Belisarius sat waiting to receive the Goths, on a high chair flanked by twenty guardsmen. Antonina sat on a smaller chair to his left, lovely as ever. Photius stood behind her, rigid and upright, silver breastplate shining like a freshly minted coin, his plumed helmet tucked underarm.

I felt an irrational twinge of jealousy. It had once been my duty to guard the general, but he had chosen to set me aside. The sight of Antonina made me wonder if my dismissal from the Guards had been her doing. Perhaps she thought I was too close to her husband, and had to be removed in case I influenced him against her.

The hall rang to the chatter of the assembled senators and lesser dignitaries. Their voices died away when Belisarius raised his arm for silence.

"Come forward," he said, beckoning the chief envoy, "and state your case. King Vitiges asked for this meeting to take place. We pray that he has sent you with reasonable terms to lay before us."

The envoy, also the tallest and most richly-dressed of the Goths, swaggered forward and gave the most perfunctory of bows.

"My royal master sends greetings, Flavius Belisarius," he boomed, "and congratulates you on the victories you have won so far. Your Emperor is wise and fortunate in his choice of generals."

Belisarius bowed his head to acknowledge the compliment.

"No general, however skilled and favoured by God," the Goth continued, "could hope to prevail against such overwhelming odds as are now stacked against you. Rome is invested from all sides. You have no hope of relief from Constantinople. My master charges you not to prolong the sufferings of the citizens of Rome, who for long have prospered under the beneficent rule of our kings."

He turned and spread his brawny arms to address the senators. "Have my people not made Rome great again?" he demanded, "have we not lifted her from the pit of shame and ruin she had fallen into, under the tyranny of your degenerate Emperors? Senators, the time of the Caesars is long past. The last Emperor of the West died in exile, and his regalia lies in a vault in Constantinople. Why, then, did you open your gates to receive Belisarius and his army of hirelings? Why do you choose the slavery that Justinian would subject you to, over the enlightened rule of the Goths?"

A white-bearded senator stepped forward to speak, but Belisarius waved him back.

"I speak for the people of Rome," the general said in a voice that brooked no protest, "and I will tell you why the Romans admitted us. They know we are engaged in a national and rightful cause. Rome does not belong to your barbarian kings, no matter how wisely and well they might rule the city. Should we applaud a thief for spending the treasures he steals on worthy causes? He is still a thief. My master is the direct heir of Romulus Augustus, the last Emperor of the West, and has sent me to reclaim his inheritance."

The envoy clasped his hands together and gave a sorrowful little shake of his head. "King Vitiges feared that would be your reply. If you are so bent on your own destruction, he begs you to think of the people of Rome, and not seek to hide any longer behind their walls. He challenges you, Belisarius, to march out with all your army and meet us in open battle. If, however, you prefer the path of reason, and agree to surrender, you and your men will be permitted to depart from Italy in peace."

"Your king savours a victory he has not yet won," Belisarius replied in a tone of amused contempt, "my system of warfare shall be guided, not by his judgment or yours, but by my own. Far from viewing my prospects with any gloomy forebodings, I tell you that the time will come, when, reduced to your last detachment, driven from your last camp, you shall seek and scarcely find a refuge in bushes and brambles. If any one of your soldiers thinks to enter Rome, without fighting for every foot of ground, and meeting with the most determined resistance, he shall find himself grievously mistaken. So long as Belisarius lives, expect no surrender."

It was a fine speech, and drew a smattering of applause from the onlookers. Not for the first time, it struck me that Belisarius cut a regal figure, far more so than his master, and was fitter to rule an empire than serve one.

The envoy made no reply to this defiance, but turned and swept out at the head of his comrades, his bearded face suffused with rage.

"That's it, then," said Procopius, delicately stepping aside as the Goths barged past, "war to the knife, and may God have pity on the loser."

16.

If Belisarius' defiant response was intended to drive the Goths into a fury, then it succeeded. Very soon after their envoys had returned to repeat the general's word to Vitiges, they started making preparations for an all-out assault on the walls.

They worked, day and night, to construct siege engines. Four mighty wooden towers, each larger than the one that had guarded the Milvian Bridge, built on gigantic rollers. Dozens of scaling ladders, and great piles of faggots and reeds to fill up the ditch when they attacked, and four battering rams. These last were the most impressive, and the most terrifying.

The rams were made of several tree trunks bound together and topped with a lump of iron crudely forged into the form of a ram's head, complete with curling horns. They were placed on timber carriages with four wheels, and pushed by no less than fifty men inside a covered compartment at the base.

"Some barbarians, eh?" said Procopius as we stood on the western wall one evening and watched this frightful arsenal take shape, "it seems Belisarius has woken a bear from its slumber."

Meantime Belisarius was far from idle. His workmen laboured feverishly to build war-machines. Onagri, a kind of mechanical sling for hurling rocks, were mounted on the towers, alongside ballistae, large crossbows capable of shooting darts the size of lances, powerful enough to pierce wood or even stone.

One of his engineers devised a particularly fearsome machine called a lupus to defend the city gates. This consisted of a thick wooden beam with holes bored into it, suspended over the archway of a gate. A lattice of sharpened iron spikes was held above the beam, and dropped through the holes when an enemy passed underneath, impaling him.

At daybreak on the thirtieth day of March, eighteen days after the beginning of the siege, the Gothic host broke camp and advanced to attack the Salarian Gate, on the northern side of the city. Vitiges appeared to have history in mind, for this was the same gate via which his famous forebear, Alaric, had forced entry into Rome over two hundred years previously.

Belisarius crammed as many fighting men as possible on the walls flanking the semi-circular towers of the gatehouse, with reserves deployed in the streets below. I and the remaining Heruls under my command were among the men on the wall, where we enjoyed (if that is the right word) a spectacular view of the advancing host.

I have mentioned that Procopius was no soldier, but he had found a helmet and a breastplate from somewhere, neither of which fitted him, and joined us on the walls. He was armed with his long knife, which I suspected he knew how to use, and a spear, which I was certain he didn't.

"What a sight!" he exclaimed, lifting the rim of his oversized helmet to stare, pop-eyed, with genuine delight at the teeming squadrons of Goths.

His voice was almost drowned by the hellish din of their advance: thousands of marching feet, the deep, drawn-out booming of their bull-horns, their guttural prayers and war-songs, the thunder of drums and squalling trumpets.

I made no answer, incapable of tearing my eyes from the monstrous ram wheeling slowly towards the gate. The other three were lined up in a row behind it, ready to be pushed forward if the first failed in its task.

As for the main part of the Gothic army, the sight of those legions converging on Rome has haunted my nightmares for the best part of thirty years. It seemed to me that they needed no ladders or war-engines – that great boiling mass of bodies could simply pour over our flimsy defences and suffocate us with sheer weight of numbers.

"Courage, Romans! Have no fear of these barbarian animals! Cast your javelins at them, shower them with arrows and rocks and boiling oil! Send them fleeing back to the northern wastelands that birthed them!"

Belisarius' voice rose above the tumult. His words put fresh heart into our soldiers. The ballistae and onagri on the towers hurled their missiles into the densely-packed enemy ranks, flattening scores of warriors and impaling others. I gave a savage cheer as I witnessed one bolt drive clean through a spearman's breast, burst from his spine and transfix three men behind him.

It was now that I saw Belisarius snatch a bow from an Isaurian archer, take careful aim, and put an arrow through the neck of a Gothic officer. Our soldiers gave a great shout when they witnessed this exploit. Belisarius promptly took another arrow from the grinning Isaurian's quiver and repeated the feat.

"Shoot the oxen!" he commanded, and our archers lining the walls bent their bows and let fly. They aimed at the beasts pulling the four siege towers rumbling towards the city, and within moments their targets crumpled to the ground. The towers stopped dead, and Procopius howled with laughter at the confusion on the faces of the Gothic soldiers packed inside.

"Look at those stupid Germanic pigs!" he cackled, forgetting that half our own men were Germans, "they spent days building those big towers, and didn't think to put some armour on the oxen. Fresh cows needed, brother Herman!"

His laughter was short-lived. The towers were rendered immobile, but the ram continued to rumble on towards the gate. Belisarius screamed at our archers to fell the men pushing it, but most of the arrows rebounded or struck harmlessly on the thick coverings of ox-hide the Goths had stretched over the compartment at the base.

Some of the Isaurians were supplied with rags dipped in oil, and had lit braziers ready to set the rags on fire after they were wrapped around the tips of their arrows.

The fire-arrows had been intended to set the Gothic towers ablaze, but now their officers ordered them used against the ram.

It worked. The ox-hide was dry as tinder, and the flames quickly took hold. Most of the men cowering inside abandoned the ram and fled into the open, where our bowmen had great sport picking them off.

Now the great swarm of Gothic infantry broke into a charge. Our archers mowed them down as they struggled across the ditch, filling the freshly-dug trenches with twitching bodies. Their comrades clambered over the dead and wounded, or filled the ditch with heaps of faggots and reeds to act as rough bridges.

"Let them burn!" roared Belisarius, and the Isaurians poured their flaming arrows into the ditch, setting the dry reeds alight.

The flames turned that ditch into Hell on earth, through which the Goths struggled, screaming as they burned alive. Many of them suffocated, trampled by their fellows, but still the rest bravely came on.

So much wasted courage. The few that managed to cross the ditch and reach the foot of the walls were exposed to javelins, rocks and hot oil dropped on them from above.

Every man on the wall was supplied with three javelins apiece. I cast the first of mine at a Goth just as he glanced upwards. The slender iron-tipped missile passed straight through his gaping mouth and out the back of his neck.

"Well struck!" cried Procopius, his voice shrill with excitement, "give me one of your javelins, Coel, and let me fell one of the bastards."

I handed him one, and laughed at his clumsy attempt at a throw. The javelin flew well wide of any Goths and stuck, quivering, in the earth.

"Another!" he demanded, but I was distracted by a sound of a trumpet.

I looked down and saw Constantine standing in the street. His helmet was dented, and his breastplate smeared with blood. He had a desperate, wild look in his eyes, and waved his arms frantically at me.

"The Goths!" he shouted, "they are inside the city! My men cannot hold them!"

Constantine, I remembered, had been entrusted with guarding the north-eastern quarter. His troops were stationed at Hadrian's mausoleum on the south side of the Tiber.

The noise of battle was deafening, and only I and a few other men on the walls had heard him. I risked a charge of desertion if I abandoned my post, but Constantine was clearly in dire need of reinforcements.

"Follow!" I yelled in the ear of one of my Heruls. He passed the word to his comrades, and I led them down the steps to the street. A few others, no more than a dozen or so, trailed after us.

"Coel," Constantine said warmly, gripping my wrist, "I knew you would not fail me. Come, we must hurry."

We raced through the streets, heading towards the sepulchre of the Emperor Hadrian. The enormous silhouette rose above the ramparts and dominated the skyline in that part of the city.

The sepulchre consisted of a massive square base, with a circular mole, about a thousand feet in circumference and made of great blocks of white marble. Its base was adorned with statues of gods and equestrian figures worked in bronze and marble, and the whole surrounded by a paved sidewalk and a railing of gilt bronze, supported by pillars crowned with gilded peacocks.

Appropriate to the memory of the great soldier-emperor whose remains were housed inside, it served as a fortress as well as mausoleum, and was connected to part of the outer defences.

"The Goths hid beneath the Church of Saint Peter," Constantine breathlessly explained as we ran, "my attention was called away to another part of the walls, and I left just a few men to guard the mausoleum. Suddenly the enemy poured out of hiding and rushed the defences."

The Church of Saint Peter lay outside the circuit of the walls, within a stone's throw of the mausoleum. Some clever Gothic officer must have had the idea of concealing some of his men in the arcades and porticoes of the church, while the others were sent to draw away the defenders.

Constantine had left his men to hold off the Goths while he went in search of reinforcements. The sound of fighting grew louder as we raced over Hadrian's bridge and through the archway into the vestibule, a great square chamber dominated by an equestrian statue of Hadrian. His stern, bearded features seemed to glower in disapproval at us as we ascended the spiral stair leading to the central chamber.

Constantine was first through the narrow door that led onto the roof, where his men were struggling to hold back waves of Goths. The enemy had laid ladders against the outer wall of the mausoleum, and were swarming up them in their hundreds. Constantine's Huns and Isaurians had thrown down some of the ladders, and littered the ground below with Gothic corpses, but there was no end to the brutes.

He ran to aid his men, locked in vicious combat on the western side of the base. It was obvious they could not hold for much longer. They had already suffered terrible casualties, were out of arrows and javelins, and exposed to the Gothic archers below.

I hesitated to join the fray. My six Heruls were not likely to make much difference, and I was reluctant to waste lives to no purpose.

One of my men – Ubaz, I think his name was – pointed his sword at one of the bronze statues. He had no need to speak, for the same idea had already occurred to me.

"With me!" I yelled at the others, and all seven of us ran to the statue and knelt to seize its legs.

"Ready – lift!" We put our shoulders to the task and lifted it a few inches off the floor. The damned thing was crushingly heavy, even with seven of us, and I bit my lip as fresh pain scorched through my bad shoulder.

Grunting and cursing, we shuffled sideways, crab-like, across the roof. Constantine had seen us, and shouted at his men to clear a path.

I peered down at the teeming mass of Goths below the wall, shouted "heave!" and with a final effort we pitched the statue over the edge.

It was some eight feet high, and I like to think that the long-dead sculptor who shaped it would have had no objection to his creation being used as a missile against invading barbarians. Horse and rider plunged down onto the heads of a band of Goths clustered at the base of a scaling ladder, who looked up just in time to see the fatal shadow descending on them. The screams that rose in their throats were cut off, suddenly and satisfyingly, and replaced by a grisly squelch.

"Fetch more!" Constantine roared, and a number of his men ran to pick up more of the statues that crowned the base. Some, such as the statues of Apollo and Venus and other pagan deities from Rome's distant past, were lighter than others, and could be carried by just two or three men.

Within moments the bemused Goths found themselves being pelted with statuary. I later heard a poet declare, much to the disapproval of the priests, that Rome's ancient gods had come to life to protect the city, where they were had been worshipped and adored before the arrival of Christ. It was a nice image, but the hands that threw down the statues were entirely mortal.

The Goths panicked and scattered, ducking for cover and holding their shields above their heads. No fragile linden wood shield is proof against half a ton of marble, and before long the ground below the wall was strewn with dead men, flattened like insects under a man's heel, their bodies crushed into so much bleeding pulp.

Having almost lost Rome to the Goths, Constantine was in no mood to allow them any respite. Leaving me to hold the mausoleum, he took some thirty of his men down the stair, fetched their horses from a nearby barracks and led them out of the city via a postern gate.

I watched, panting and rubbing my aching shoulder, as his cavalry pursued the fleeing Goths, spearing them like rabbits and driving them headlong across the fields. Fresh reserves of the enemy stood waiting about a mile beyond the city, and for a moment I thought Constantine meant to lead his handful of men in a death-or-glory charge. Thankfully, he turned about and trotted back to the safety of the walls.

We had slain over two hundred Goths, for the loss of some thirty or forty of our own men. Not a bad tally, but it was nothing more than a minor victory snatched from the jaws of disaster. The thousands of Gothic reserves were unperturbed by the defeat of their fellows, and stood in disciplined squares, waiting for the order to renew the assault.

"That is twice you have come to my rescue," said Constantine when he returned from his sally, "I owe you much, Coel. Be assured that someday I will repay the debt in full."

He was the same over-earnest, slightly unsettling character I had known in Sicily. His startling blue eyes gazed at me from a mask of blood and sweat with brazen intensity.

"I have told you before, there is no debt between us," I said, disengaging my wrist with some difficulty from his clasp, "one of my men had the idea of using the statues. I have done no more than my duty to a fellow officer."

I may as well have remonstrated with the wall. He enfolded me in a bone-crushing embrace, and I might have never escaped from it had the Gothic horns not renewed their dreadful song.

"They are coming again!" he cried, pushing me away, "back to your post, Coel. We can hold them here now."

I led my Heruls back towards the Salarian Gate, none too quickly, for I was exhausted from my vigours and reluctant to risk my skin a third time. God had so far kept me safe in the battle for Rome, but a man can only stretch his luck too far.

The streets beyond the Bridge of Hadrian were all but deserted, for the terrified citizens had taken refuge inside their homes from the fury of the Goths. I took the opportunity to lean against a wall and catch my breath.

My Heruls stood around, waiting impatiently for me to recover. They were all young men, my juniors by ten years or more. Only ingrained respect for a superior officer prevented them from running back to the sound of fighting, like hares outpacing a tired old hound.

God, it seemed, intended to keep me busy that night. I had not rested for more than a few seconds when the sound of hoof beats clattering over the cobbles reached my ears, and Bessas thundered into sight, accompanied by a few troopers.

"You!" he shouted, reining in at sight of me, "to the Praenestine Gate, at once! Every man is needed there!"

He rode off without waiting to see if I followed. The Praenestine Gate was at least a mile away, in the south-eastern quarter of the city, and was part of the region called the Vivarium, where the Romans had once housed the wild beasts they kept for public entertainments.

Duty summoned me for one last effort, and so I forced my aching legs into a trot. The Heruls jogged at my side, eager for more bloodshed. They were a savage and warlike people, as I had learned in their camp outside Constantinople, and their taste for violence and fighting knew no bounds.

As we drew nearer to the Vivarium I overheard the thump and crash of artillery. The Goths were bombarding the gate and outer wall, which was lower than the inner and made of inferior quality stone, with their catapults and onagers.

The bombardment abruptly ceased, replaced almost immediately by the clash of steel and the familiar sound of men fighting and dying. We turned a corner and almost ran into a column of our soldiers, advancing at the double towards the gates.

I paused to take stock and wipe the perspiration dripping from my brow. The Vivarium consisted of an enclosure between the higher inner wall and the outer bulwark, which the Goths were attempting to storm. Our men inside the enclosure had abandoned the bulwark and retreated a few paces, where they stood at bay to repel the tide of barbarian warriors pouring over the rampart.

Bessas was riding to and fro behind the lines, shouting at our infantry to form a shield-wall. Reinforcements were hurrying towards the fray from the various smaller gates inside the inner wall. Bessas roared them into battle, and the weight of their additional numbers stiffened our sagging line and shoved the Goths back, slaughtering many and driving the survivors back over the wall.

It was a temporary respite, and the sound of those hateful bull-horns gave warning that the enemy were reforming for another assault. I offered up a quick silent prayer and led my Heruls on to take our places in the rear ranks of the shield-wall Bessas was hurriedly assembling.

"Fill those gaps, there!" he yelled, his voice shrill and hoarse, "get the dead and wounded to the rear. Take a mouthful of water and pass your pottles around to those who have none. Move faster, you dogs!"

I thought it a vain effort to try and defend the outer bulwark. The wall was too low, and our numbers too few to hold it indefinitely against wave after wave of Goths. I looked around at our men, and saw only grey faces, drawn with effort and exhaustion.

There was another who agreed with me. Hoofs clattered behind me, and I looked around to see Belisarius cantering through a gate inside the inner wall, followed by a group of his officers.

The general had come straight from the battle at the Salarian Gate. He looked no less tired than anyone else, his helmet and breastplate dinted and smeared with blood, his face gaunt, heavy jaw clenched against fatigue.

He summoned Bessas to his side. The two spoke urgently, their voices too low to hear above the din of horns and war-shouts. When they were done, Belisarius wheeled his horse and disappeared through the gate, while Bessas gestured at his trumpeters.

"Withdraw!" he screamed once the shrill blast of the trumpets had died away, "abandon the wall, and form line here!"

He pointed at the foot of the inner wall. Our men shuffled backwards to reform in front of him. The manoeuvre caught me by surprise, and I was almost knocked over and trampled under the front ranks, but two of my Heruls pulled me clear. I thought I overhear one of them grumble something about looking after the old man, and shot him a venomous look.

"Throw down your javelins," Bessas ordered, "swords and shields only."

The men of the front rank did so, casting aside all their spears and javelins and drawing their swords for close combat. I stood in the third line, with Bessas just behind me, and kissed the blade of Caledfwlch for luck. There were no walls to hide behind here, no supply of statues to rain down on the enemy. We would meet the enemy to their beards and make a final stand, here, where the defences of Rome were at their weakest.

"I promised you hard service, Briton," grunted Bessas, "see you make the shades of your ancestors proud. I wager your grandsire never took a backward step."

I was flattered he even remembered who my grandsire was, and tried to will away the cramp stealing across my limbs. I could feel my strength ebbing, just when I needed it most.

We waited for what seemed an agonisingly long time. The Goths were taunting us, letting fear and doubt gnaw at our minds while they gathered their superior numbers for the final charge.

"Come on, you bastards," I heard a Hunnish spearman mutter in front of me, "let's have it over with."

I was taller than most of the Easterners that made up our infantry, and able to peer over their heads at the Gothic banners outside the bulwark. One of them was huge, a great square crimson standard fringed with gold, and with a shock I realised it was the banner of their king. Vitiges himself was present outside the Praenestine Gate. I tried to picture him, and shuddered at the image my mind conjured up of a gigantic bearded savage, red to the armpits in Roman blood and wielding a battle-axe bigger than my head.

With a final blast of horns and a mighty shout that split the night skies, they came. Their forward line of warriors leaped over the bulwark and galloped towards our line, roaring like enraged lions. Hundreds more flooded in their wake. Against this multitude our flimsy treble line of swords and shields seemed certain to break, smashed to bits and swept away, leaving Rome open to the vengeance of the Goths.

They hit us like a steel fist into an exposed gut. The big Hun standing in front of me was shoved backwards, and the back of his helm smashed into my face, breaking my nose. Tears started to my eyes. I staggered, blinded and whimpering in pain, and gasped as my spine thumped against the brickwork of the inner wall.

The Hun's crushing weight pressed against me, and for a few terrible seconds I struggled to breathe. His rank stench was in my throat and nostrils – many of our Hunnish mercenaries refused to wash, thinking that bathing sapped their strength – and I flailed my arms uselessly, almost losing my grip on Caledfwlch. The triumphant yells of the Goths churned in my ears, deafening me. I was blind, robbed of my senses, crushed and defenceless, and about to die.

The infernal howling of the Goths was drowned by a pure, rising note, like the clarion call of angels. Some of the awful pressure on my body eased, and I was able to push the Hun away. He was a dead weight, his neck chopped almost clean in two by an axe. "Let's have it done and over with," he had begged, and God granted him his wish.

The triumphant Gothic yells had turned to cries of fear and panic. Roman trumpets were sounding all over the field beyond the outer wall. Through a mist of pain I glimpsed the banners of Belisarius, illuminated in the fires lit by the Goths to aid their advance.

I was already weeping, my tears mingling with the blood trickling from the ruin of my nose, but now I wept with joy and relief as well as pain.

Belisarius had ordered Bessas to abandon the bulwark and retreat to the inner wall of the Vivarium, tempting the Goths to launch an all-out assault. Packed inside that narrow enclosure, they were taken unawares when Belisarius led his cavalry out of the neighbouring gates and fell upon them, flank and rear.

Hemmed in against our infantry, scarcely able to turn or even lift their weapons, the Goths were butchered like sheep. Unknown to me, Belisarius had also ordered his men to fire the Gothic artillery, so the scene of his victory was lit by the hellish glow of burning war-machines.

Bessas led a counter-attack, and ordered the archers and javelin-men on the walls above us to hurl their missiles into the hapless ranks of the enemy. Our infantry surged forward with renewed vigour, and I had space and leisure to collapse to my knees and throw up.

Fortunately, Bessas was otherwise engaged, otherwise he might have witnessed me behaving in a manner that my warlike grandsire would certainly have disapproved of. After the spasms had passed, I wiped my mouth and remained on all fours, debating whether to feign death until the fighting was over. I had seen my limit of hard service, as Bessas might have termed it, and longed for rest and safety.

What of my men? I had not seen them since the Goths attacked. The force of responsibility overwhelmed my selfish cowardice, and I climbed wearily to my feet, Caledfwlch weighing like lead in my hand.

The enclosure was emptying now. Those Goths still alive had broken past our cavalry and were fleeing in all directions across the field, leaving great piles of their slain. Our men pursued them, or else wandered among the reeking carnage, finishing off the wounded and bending to inspect the dead for valuables. Gothic warriors, particularly the high-ranking ones, loved to decorate their bodies with gold, so there were rich pickings to be had.

My Heruls were nowhere to be seen. I imagined they were happily chasing Goths on the plain, but still felt duty-bound to go in search of them. Sighing, I started to limp towards the outer wall, when a hand fell lightly on my shoulder.

"Coel," said Belisarius, "I seem to remember we met in similar circumstances, inside the Hippodrome after the Nika riots. Do you remember?"

I turned, slowly, and dropped to one knee. "I remember, sir," I replied, bowing my head.

In truth, it was impossible to forget that ghastly, blood-soaked night when Belisarius' Veterans and Huns had made chopped liver of the Nika rioters, most of whom were civilians. I had played my part in the butchery, and when the sun finally rose over the arena, piled high with the bodies of Roman citizens, Belisarius had congratulated me and taken my oath as a soldier.

He placed his index finger under my chin and tilted my face up. I had rarely seen a man look so tired, but his mouth twitched into a smile as he studied me.

"Your nose," he said, "resembles a burst fruit. Now you have the proper appearance of a Roman officer."

He helped me to stand. "Come. My aides will take you to my quarters. You have done more than enough for one night. And keep that sword safe!"

I allowed two of his junior officers to lead me away. Purple clouds drifted before my eyes, and I could feel my legs giving way under me. I was a man of straw, buckling in the wind, and blood flowed freely from my shoulder like a torrent of wine.

Blood. Oceans of blood. It all seemed to leave my body at once, and I toppled forward into blissful nothing.

17.

"Hello, Coel," said Antonina.

The mists before my eyes cleared, and I found myself gazing at that lovely heart-shaped face, just inches from my own.

At first I thought I was dreaming. Her red lips were close enough to kiss, and I felt an impulse to reach up and stroke her cheek. She was entrancing, as desirable as she was vile. I had to have her. I had to kill her.

Reality intruded as pain flared in my shoulder. The half-healed wound was now sealed by a neat line of stitches, but it still stung as though hot knives were being pressed against my flesh.

"Lie back," she said in a warm, soothing voice, sweet as honey, deadly as poison, "you have slept for two days and nights. What injuries you have suffered on behalf of Rome. Your body is a network of scars."

I looked down, and found I was lying in a large, too-soft bed in a bedchamber fit for an empress. The walls were decorated with friezes and tapestries, and the white marble of the floor covered in costly Persian rugs.

"What in God's name…" I croaked, pulling the heavy bedclothes up to cover my naked body.

"Are you doing here, in my care?" said Antonina, smiling as she finished the sentence for me.

Her golden hair was bound up, and she was dressed like a respectable Roman matron in a white stola, a long, pleated woolen dress reaching to her ankles. The stola was sleeveless, exposing her shapely white arms.

"You fainted," she went on, frowning slightly as she inspected her stitching, "and so my husband turned you over to me. Give our fallen hero plenty of food and rest, he said, and also sent a doctor to look at your wounds. I dismissed the man. Like most military physicians, he was a butcher, and would have bled and purged you to death. I tell you, Coel, I have more knowledge of the art of healing in my little finger."

I eyed her with loathing. Two days and nights in the care of Antonina, one of my most dangerous enemies. She might have easily murdered me as I slept, and yet I still lived.

Caledfwlch. Where was my sword? I looked around frantically, and spotted it standing on top of a neatly-folded pile of clean clothing on a chair.

"Have no fear," said Antonina, with the mannered little laugh, devoid of any true mirth, that I remembered from our brief encounter in Carthage, "I am no thief. Old Julius's sword is your rightful property, everyone knows that."

I had nothing to say to her, and was determined to be up and out of her bedchamber as quickly as possible.

"I have men outside," she said as I made to throw back the bedclothes, "you can depart when I give you permission, not before."

Her light, playful voice had suddenly acquired an edge. I hesitated, watching her closely.

What game was she playing? Antonina had tried to seduce me in Carthage, in a failed attempt to damn me in the eyes of her husband. She was hand-in-glove with Theodora, the Empress who had conspired to make me fight for my life in the Hippodrome.

Her foul son, Photius, had tried to kill me at Membresa, almost certainly on her orders. I had little doubt that she was also behind the latest attempt on my life, beneath the aqueduct outside Napoli.

"You are wondering," she said complacently, "why I have chosen to spare your life, when I could have taken it at any time during the past two days."

I said nothing. The subtleties of this woman were beyond me, but I knew what she was capable of, and that any word that fell from my mouth would be deliberated twisted and misconstrued.

She cocked her head to one side. "Lost your tongue? Heavens, Coel, you look like a frightened mouse. I do believe you are more afraid of me than any raging Gothic swordsman."

"You need not be afraid. Why should I wish to rub out our tough little Briton? I enjoy watching you too much. Holding onto that absurd sword like a baby with a rattle, forcing yourself to fight and play the hero, creeping around underground passages…always surrounded by death and danger, always alone, suspicious, scared, tossed about like a straw on the seas of fate."

This was too much. I felt compelled to speak. "You will get nothing from me, lady," I said, sitting up, "so you may as well let me go, or call in your men to murder me. Just as you ordered your son to murder me at Membresa."

She pushed back a loose strand of hair. "Photius is a disappointment," she replied, "though admittedly I have not been much of a mother to him. I was not born to be a parent. He was an accident. Perhaps I shouldn't have told him that quite so often."

Notice how she avoided the issue. She made no effort to excuse or explain Photius' attempt to kill me. Nor was I interested in listening to her lies.

"I have some good news for you," she said, "my husband was greatly impressed by your recent heroics in the defence of Rome. He means to promote you again. To centenar."

My head still felt as though it was stuffed with wool. I gaped stupidly at her, struggling to comprehend.

"Your Heruls are all dead," she added casually, "killed in the fighting by the Praenestine Gate. Some might question why Belisarius wishes to put an officer who wastes the lives of ten men in charge of a hundred, but of course I know nothing of soldiering."

"Dead?" I gasped. Antonina had completely wrong-footed me now. She was enjoying herself immensely, batting me back and forth in her paws, like a cat with a dazed mouse.

"Yes, all quite dead. Don't be too sad about it, Coel. They fought well, by all accounts, if unwisely. Of course they had no officer on hand to restrain them."

She gave a little shrug of her delectable shoulders. "Soldiers die, especially if they are Heruls. Those savages believe it a great dishonour to die anywhere save the battlefield."

I kindled with anger. "I know rather more about the customs of the Heruls than you, lady," I said, "their deaths are on my conscience. Why do you taunt me with them? Is this how you derive your pleasures?"

"What a bore you are, Coel," she said, with a little yawn, "Theodora warned me that you are a bore. Your life could have been so different, so much easier and more rewarding, if only you had submitted to my friend's desires."

She referred to my refusal to take part in a three-way coupling with the Empress, during an orgy in Constantinople, and my later refusal to spy on Belisarius during the North African campaign. I had never regretted either decision, though they cost me the life of a childhood friend, and caused me much pain and hardship since.

"You are proud, of course," she went on, "ever so proud of your descent from barbarian princes and a remarkable grandfather. Arthur, was his name? I think I can picture him. An uncouth Roman-British chieftain, covered in tattoos and war-paint, strong as an ox, smelly as a pig."

Now I understood. Antonina was trying to goad me, to provoke me into reaching for Caledfwlch and striking her down. As soon as I moved, she would yell for her guards and have me cut to pieces on the spot. Like her friend Theodora, she was not half so subtle as she pretended, and every bit as murderous.

"I imagine he held court in a big wooden hall," she went on, warming to her theme, "with straw and dung on the floors and shields hanging on the walls. His warriors got swine-drunk on mead and boasted to each other of the men they had killed. The great man himself sat at high table, drinking bad wine and wearing a purple-dyed cloak in a pitiful attempt at aping Roman customs and styles. A stinking, ignorant, ludicrous barbarian."

She had some strange notions of British fashions – only the wild Picts beyond the Wall painted their bodies – and I was more amused than offended.

"Arthur would have been a barbarian to your eyes, true," I replied, "but he had honour, and courage, and fought to the last to defend his country. He killed his enemies face-to-face, on the battlefield, and never stooped to conspiring in dark corners, or sending hired murderers to do his dirty work. Where is Elene?"

Antonina waved aside my feeble effort to throw her off-track. "Honour," she mused, "what a strange notion. Men spend their time killing each other like beasts in the field, and so invented the rules of honour to make it all more seemly. I am but a weak woman, Coel, and I came from nothing. I cannot rely on a proud lineage to protect me, or pick up a sword to defend myself."

"You have plenty to do that for you," I said, with a meaningful glance at the door.

Antonia smiled again, exposing perfect white teeth, and this time her smile had a genuine warmth to it. "Perhaps you are not quite such a bore," she said, "there is a spark of wit buried away in you somewhere, under all that stiffness and stuffed nobility."

She suddenly rose and clapped her hands. The double doors swung open, and three helmed and mailed guardsmen strode in. Cursing, for Antonina had lulled me into lowering my guard, I scrambled out of bed and lunged for Caledfwlch.

My leg got tangled up in a blanket, and I missed, overturning the chair and spilling the contents all over the floor.

"For God's sake," Antonina said distastefully as I groveled on the floor, trying to kick my leg free, "do you think I intend to have you butchered in my own bedchamber? Even the Goths are more sophisticated than that. Get up and dress, you strange man. My guards have no more desire to see your naked backside than I do."

Reddening, I dragged on the underclothes, breeches, tunic and boots laid aside for me – they were new and clean, and a gift from Antonina – and wrestled on my sword-belt. There was a fine woolen cloak as well, fastened at the shoulder with a silver brooch worth more than a month's pay.

"There," she said when I was done, looking at me with a critical eye, "you are almost presentable. Not quite good enough to be presented to an emperor, but good enough for my husband. Come."

I eyed her guards suspiciously, but they seemed to have no immediate intent to murder me. Keeping my hand near Caledfwlch, I followed Antonina into the corridor.

She led me along the wide, airy passage and down a flight of steps. Her guards marched behind us, and I was painfully aware of my back being exposed to their swords, should their mistress choose to put aside her friendly mask.

The stair led to a little antechamber, which itself opened out on the grand audience chamber where I had witnessed Belisarius reject the Gothic peace terms. It was virtually empty, save for the general himself, Bessas and Constantine, and a couple of Roman senators.

They were deep in argument when we entered, their wrangling voices echoing around the hall. Antonina lifted her hand, signaling us to halt, and a smile played around her lips as she listened to the furious exchange.

"We did not ask you to come," cried one of the senators, a fleshy-faced greybeard who sprayed spittle as he talked, "Rome had recovered some of her wealth and dignity under the Goths, and her people were content. Then your Emperor saw fit to send you, General Belisarius, to drag us back into the Empire, almost a century after we had been cast adrift."

Belisarius listened impatiently, resting his chin on his fist and tapping his knee. The greybeard's companion, an enormously large man who I can best compare to a mound of rancid butter poured into a toga, took up the cudgels.

"We invited you in!" he barked, raising one fat finger in admonition, "despite the risk to her newfound peace and prosperity, Rome opened her gates to your army. The sight of imperial banners reminded us of our ancient heritage, and stirred up old passions that were best left dormant."

He stabbed the finger at Belisarius. "Now war has come, and you won't allow us to fight. Instead you put your trust in mercenaries, barbarians of mongrel blood from far-flung provinces that once paid us tribute, and you think them more fit to defend Rome than its own citizens!"

This was something new. Thus far the people of Rome had played no part in the siege, other than to irritate and harass our troops as we rebuilt the defences. The cowardly attitude of the citizens, who were after all descended from that extraordinary, all-conquering race who once made the whole world their slave, had disappointed and baffled me. How could they, with such a proud heritage, ignore a chance to throw off their Germanic masters and become true Romans again?

Now, it seemed, the victories of Belisarius had ignited a flame in their breasts. He, however, was having none of it.

"I am impressed with your valour," he said quietly once the lips of the senators had ceased to flap, "and happy to know that something of the old Roman martial spirit survives. But we must be practical. Even if I submitted to your request, and put every able-bodied man in Rome under arms, our combined army would still lack the numbers to face the Goths in open battle."

The senators squawked and scoffed at his caution. "Lack the numbers?" cried the greybeard, "why, any one of your soldiers is worth ten of those barbarians! Your generals inform me that upwards of thirty thousand Goths died in the battle three nights ago, for the loss of some three or four thousand of our men."

"My men," Belisarius corrected him, "and even if the figure of thirty thousand is accurate, that still leaves us with a hundred and twenty thousand Goths to contend with. Their Frankish allies and auxiliaries from Dalmatia will soon arrive to make good their losses."

He spread his hands. "I have written to the Emperor in Constantinople, begging him for reinforcements. So far I have received nothing in reply. Until fresh troops arrive, assuming they ever do, I cannot afford to risk the few I have in an uncertain and unnecessary battle."

"That is my reply," he said firmly when they made to protest, "tell the Senate. Good day, gentlemen."

The senators didn't like it, but there was nothing they could do, and Belisarius refused to brook any further argument. They bowed, their eyes glittering with malice, and waddled out of the room, muttering darkly to each other.

Belisarius puffed out his cheeks and slumped in his chair. Bessas spotted us, and leaned down to whisper in his ear.

He suddenly came to life again. His eyes widened as they drank in Antonina, who was already advancing towards him. She swayed slightly as she walked, and I was hard-put not to fasten my eyes on that slender, elegant frame, carved and shaped by nature to entrap men and bend them to her will. She was always a greater natural beauty than her friend Theodora, whose physical charms coarsened with age, and had to be sustained and to some extent replaced by cosmetics.

It worried me to see the light in Belisarius' eyes, which shone for no-one on earth save his wife. He was Antonina's slave, and guided by her in most things save the waging of war. His generals would have lost all respect for him if they thought his strategy was being dictated by his wife, and she was careful never to intervene.

I had rarely observed the couple at such close quarters. It struck me how she wouldn't let him get too near, warding off his embrace and kissing him chastely on the cheek.

"Coel," he said, noticing me for the first time, "back on your feet, I see. My wife has taken good care of you, then?"

"The best, sir," I replied, swallowing the bile that rose in my throat, "my shoulder is on the mend at last."

"Shame about your face, though," he said with a grin. I had forgotten my broken nose, and carefully raised my hand to touch it. The damned thing had set awkwardly. Later, when I had leisure to peer at my reflection in a mirror made of polished metal, I found that my face, never my most attractive feature, now resembled that of an African ape.

"We overheard your conversation with the senators, husband," said Antonina, "it seems they have found their courage at last."

"Fools," he growled, "they want me to arm the citizens and lead them out to face the Goths in the open. Our recent successes have convinced them that Vitiges will take one look at their swords and run away."

"If the Romans want to fight, let them," said Bessas, "but without our aid. This city would be a lot easier to defend without the inhabitants whining and snapping at us."

"Rome emptied of Romans," said Belisarius, rubbing his chin, "an attractive thought, though it would render our mission rather pointless."

He turned back to me. "Forgive me, Coel. We are neglecting you. Has my wife informed you of your promotion?"

"The Lady Antonia was good enough to do so, sir," I said woodenly, deliberately avoiding Antonina's eye. I knew she was smirking, and longed to do or say something to wipe out her insufferable complacency, "though I hardly think I deserve such an honour. You made me a decanus, and I lost my entire command."

"That was none of your fault," said Belisarius, "we lost over six hundred men at the Praenestine Gate. Many officers and men died. Your conduct, however, was exemplary. You fought at the Salarian Gate, in the defence of Hadrian's mausoleum, and at the Praenestine Gate. Constantine assures me that the Goths would have taken the mausoleum, if you had not thought to use the statuary to repel them."

Using the statues as missiles had in fact been Ubaz's idea, but he was no longer alive to claim the credit. I glanced at Constantine. At first I thought my unlooked-for promotion was mainly thanks to him, but then I received praise from an unexpected quarter.

"I saw Coel stand his ground in the last fight," said Bessas, his craggy face twisted into something like a smile, "even though he was exhausted and nigh-dead on his feet. I have no hesitation in approving his promotion."

I only stood my ground because I was pinned to the wall by a dead Hun, but it seemed impolitic to say so. God had seen fit to smile on me, which made a pleasant change from what he usually dropped on my head, and so I ate up the honey while it lasted.

18.

The siege wore on into spring. Neither side wished to risk another engagement. We could not afford the casualties, and Vitiges' already dented prestige might not have survived another defeat. The Goths only respect strength in their kings, and expect them to provide victory after victory in the field. To be repeatedly defeated by a handful of inbred Romans and ill-disciplined Eastern mercenaries, as they perceived us, was an intolerable humiliation.

Vitiges settled down to break our resistance through famine and blockade. He failed, however, to cut off the lines of communication between Rome and the Campanian coast, and in the latter days of April wonderful news arrived: a Roman fleet had arrived at last from Constantinople, carrying a squadron of Hunnish and Sclavonian cavalry.

The troops had embarked at the end of the previous year, but storms had delayed the fleet's departure and forced it to winter in Greece. They landed on the northern bank of the mouth of the Tiber, guarded by a fortress called the Port of Rome. The fort, along with the fortified town of Ostia on the southern bank, had once guarded the sea-passage into Rome, but the Goths had seized both. Even so, our reinforcements were able to get past the defences and ride along the ancient stone highway, eighteen miles in length, to the gates of the city.

Our elation was short-lived. "Is that all?" exclaimed Procopius as we watched the riders enter the Salarian Gate, "a few hundred light cavalry? There must be more!"

There were sixteen hundred in total, mostly horse-archers. They were a useful addition to our depleted garrison, but the sense of disappointment was palpable. Whether through envy or neglect or sheer poverty of resources, the Emperor had responded to Belisarius' begging letters by sending a bare minimum of aid.

Procopius, never Justinian's greatest admirer, was beside himself with rage. "He wants Belisarius to fail," he snarled, "the flatterers and traitors at court have poured so many lies into him, he can scarcely tell truth from falsehood any more. That evil whore of a wife has corrupted him with every form of degenerate vice. I tell you, Coel, Justinian is not fit to be called Caesar. He is not fit for anything save emptying the dung-pits of his slaves!"

I clapped my hand over his mouth. We were standing in the street just inside the gate, where anyone might hear us, and Procopius had just uttered enough treason to condemn him several times over.

"For God's sake, mind your tongue," I whispered, "if Belisarius overheard half of that, he would have no choice but to place you on trial. Do you want to hang?"

"Belisarius would not lay a finger on me," he sneered, pushing me away, "I know too much, and am far too valuable to him. Besides, I am sure he shares my opinion of our beloved ruler."

"Has he actually said as much?"

"Not as such, but I know him, Coel. I have been his private secretary for many years, and I can read his thoughts. It wouldn't take much for…"

His voice trailed away, thank the Lord. Even he baulked at voicing the unspeakable, though I had occasionally heard our men talking of it in low voices when in their cups.

Why were they fighting against desperate odds in the service of a distant Emperor who sent them little help, and who appeared not to care if his soldiers lived or died? Who was their real leader, the man who fought and suffered alongside them, who had led them to one improbable victory after another?

Belisarius, of course. Why could the soldiers not raise a general to the purple, instead of Justinian? It had happened before, many times, during the turbulent years when the Roman Empire tore itself apart. Unlike Justinian, who sat idle in Constantinople and lived in luxury while his people suffered, Belisarius was the very image of a soldier-emperor, in the mould of Hadrian and Trajan and Marcus Aurelius.

My history was patchy, but I seemed to recall that very few emperors whose authority relied on the army lasted very long. Being a learned historian, Procopius was well aware of this, but even he was starting to indulge treasonous thoughts. They would curdle over the years, until his brilliant mind became tragically unhinged, and he wrote a series of disgraceful secret histories damning Justinian and his court in the most lurid and ridiculous terms. The histories were hidden, for once published his life would have been forfeit. I read a few fragments, and am very thankful they remain locked away in some obscure vault. May they never, God willing, see the light of day.

Enraged at the ease with which our reinforcements had slipped past his outposts, Vitiges tightened his grip on Rome. His fleet blockaded the seas, and he made great efforts to cut off all contact between the city and our garrisons in the south. To that end he seized two ruined aqueducts which lay seven miles from Rome, the arches of which covered a substantial part of the country. His workmen turned these ruins into a makeshift fortress, blocking up the gaps with stone and clay, and inside it he placed a garrison of seven thousand men.

We were now surrounded on all sides. With every day that passed, our supplies were reduced, and fresh Gothic reinforcements were seen on the horizon. As Belisarius had predicted, his Frankish allies had sent thousands of auxiliaries to aid Vitiges, and more troops were pouring in from Dalmatia and other Gothic provinces.

The atmosphere inside the city grew desperate. Even Belisarius' ingenious water-mills could not replenish our dwindling supplies of grain, and he was forced to halve the bread ration doled out to the citizens. Any civilization is only a few meals away from collapse, and the people of Rome were already demoralised by the long months of siege and Belisarius' refusal to let them fight.

In their extremity, the Romans started to forget Christ and revert to their ancient gods and pagan idolatries. I watched in disbelief as people sought comfort from a particularly shameless breed of charlatan known as soothsayers, who claimed to be able to read the future in mystic omens and the spilled guts of animals.

"It's all harmless enough," Procopius assured me as we walked the streets together one afternoon, "let them believe in their omens and auguries. Such heathen antics are to be deplored, of course, but anything that keeps the mob quiet must also be tolerated."

I was off-duty, and inclined to spend most of my few leisure hours in his company. His lively conversation made a welcome change from attempting to communicate with the men of my new command, a hundred rough Isaurian spearmen from the wildest and most lawless regions of their native mountains. Belisarius had seen fit to put me in charge of a detachment of infantry, either because he didn't trust me with cavalry, or because there was nothing else available. I preferred to believe the latter.

We were walking near the Forum, the large rectangular plaza in the centre of Rome, surrounded by various splendid temples and government buildings. There were a number of soothsayers at large, emaciated men and women in patched robes, loudly proclaiming their nonsense while groups of wide-eyed, half-starved citizens looked on in fear and wonder, devouring every word.

I stopped to observe a particularly large crowd gathered in front of one of the temples. It was a small, square monument to Janus, the two-faced god who looks to the future and the past, with ornate decorations on the roof, a latticed window and double doors made of rusted iron to front and rear. A garland of twisted rope hung over the doors at the front.

"The doors to the Temple of Janus have been closed for centuries," said Procopius, "it used to be the custom that they would stand open in times of war, and were closed in times of peace. Rome was usually at war with someone, so they more or less always stood open."

Some demagogue was standing on an upturned barrel beside the doorway, screaming at the crowd to break the garland and smash the doors open.

"The fortunes of war have turned against us!" he bawled, spraying the mob with spittle, "and why, has this happened? Because we turned away from the old gods, who once watched over Rome during the high days of the Caesars, when our great city was the centre and heartbeat of the world!"

Some of the like-minded souls in the crowd cheered, and he raised his fist in salute. "For too long has the statue of Janus sat in darkness! He presides over the beginning and ending of wars, and there shall be no end to this war unless we open these doors and allow light into his temple!"

The mob surged forward and ripped away the garland, tearing it to pieces and stamping on it. Some of them wielded hammers and picks – I suspected that this little demonstration had been arranged beforehand – and started beating at the rusted iron doors.

"This is against the law, you know," said Procopius, "the worship of pagan idols was abolished when the Empire formally adopted Christianity. If an officer of the law was present, he would have no choice but to arrest the culprits."

He gave me a sly look. As a soldier, it was technically my duty to enforce the laws. I was also the only soldier in sight, and had no intention of risking my neck by standing between the Romans and their absurd deities.

In any case, the doors were rusted firmly shut, and stood up against their blows. Janus remained in darkness, and for all I know still sits inside his little temple, neglected and forgotten, biding his time until the light of Christ fades from the world and men turn back to the old ways.

There was no end to the trouble caused by these Romans, who we had been sent to rescue from barbarian slavery. Their senators, urged on by the mass of the people, continued to harass Belisarius, pleading with him to let them march out and confront the Goths. Some of his officers added their voices to the chorus, arguing that the Goths would not expect us to sally out in force.

If our men, who should have known better, had kept quiet, then Belisarius might have safely ignored the yelping of the Romans. As it was, he started to buckle. This alarmed me, for the last time he yielded to the protests of others, and gave battle against his better judgment, was at Callinicum against the Sassanids. That battle had ended in defeat, though Belisarius managed to stage a fighting retreat and save the greater part of the Roman army.

At last my fears were realised. Belisarius gave way to these combined demands, and declared his intention to march out in force and attack the Goths.

19.

Belisarius was cautious, else I would not be here now, blinking wearily at this parchment and praying for strength to ignore the rheumatic pains in my wrist. My candle burns low, and the shadows lengthen.

The general split his army in two. Led by himself, the main part sallied out of the Pincian and Salarian gates to engage the Gothic troops north of the city, while a band of cavalry under two officers named Valerian and Martinus attacked the Goths encamped west of the Tiber, on the Plains of Nero, to prevent them helping their comrades to the north.

These men were reinforced by the Roman citizens, a disorderly rabble of poorly-armed militia, and a detachment of Moorish cavalry. Belisarius did what he could to ensure that the Romans came to no harm, and gave them strict orders to act as a last-ditch reserve. They were to take up position to the rear, at the foot of the city walls, and not move unless the officers summoned them.

Belisarius spent the morning arranging his men near the gates, but waited until after midday before ordering the attack. The century of Isaurians in my charge were part of his main army, again under the overall command of Bessas, who seemed to have taken a liking to me.

Unlike the Heruls, I had little in common with the Isaurians, who I found to be sullen and intractable, and fond of playing at dumb insolence when I gave them orders. They made great play of struggling to understand my accent, cupping their ears and exchanging baffled glances when I addressed them.

At last, on the evening before the battle, I lost patience and had the chief offender tied to a barrel and flogged by two of his comrades until the blood flowed down his hairy back. After that, they seemed to regard me with a degree of grudging respect, and I felt a little more confident leading them into battle.

Cleverly, Belisarius commanded his men to stand down and take some food, hoping to deceive the Goths into thinking he had put off the attack. The ploy worked, and the Gothic squadrons arrayed for battle on the plains north of the walls started to break up.

"Open the gates!" Belisarius shouted. He and Bessas were in command of the infantry, while he had entrusted his six hundred Hunnish cavalry to a trio of officers from Persia and Thrace.

The smaller Pincian Gate was flung open, and our cavalry streamed out of the city. Bessas led the infantry through the Salarian Gate at a more orderly pace, column by column, to deploy in squadrons just beyond the outer ditch. We were not to advance, but act as a reserve to cover the retreat of our cavalry in case they were defeated and thrown back.

In truth, I doubt Belisarius had set his heart on winning that battle. The Goths were too many, and he had only consented to fight in order to prevent a mutiny among the officers and senators. He was handed a stark choice of sacrificing the lives of his men in order to please their vanity, or refusing their demands and risking a full-scale revolt.

His leadership and authority were on a knife-edge at all times, just one wrong decision removed from catastrophe. Such had the ancient Roman virtues of discipline and respect for higher authority fallen away in these degenerate latter days.

I was privileged, if that is the word, to observe a battle from afar rather than risking my neck in the midst of one.

All went well for a time. Our Hunnish and Sclavonian horse-archers skillfully charged and retreated, avoiding contact with the superior numbers of Gothic lancers and spearmen and showering them with arrows. Despite their appalling losses, the Goths held their line and refused to advance. They had learned to be wary of Belisarius, and feared moving forward in case they fell into some clever ambush.

There was no ambush. Belisarius' one aim was to kill as many Goths as possible before ordering a general advance. Sweat clouded my eyes and rolled down my back, already boiling inside layers of leather and mail, as I imagined our meagre squadrons being ordered forward to engage that great mass of barbarians.

If we marched onto the open plain, away from the protection of the ditch and our archers on the walls, the Gothic cavalry could easily encircle our flanks and rear, while their infantry engaged us head-on. We risked being swamped, trapped and crushed inside the closing steel jaws of the enemy.

For hours the fight raged back and forth, while the sun slowly dipped in the sky and I silently pleaded for Belisarius to change his mind and order a withdrawal.

I witnessed some extraordinary sights during the course of the fighting. Cutilas, the Thracian officer whom Belisarius had entrusted with part of the cavalry, plunged alone into the midst of a howling band of Gothic lancers, and was struck in the head by a javelin. He cut his way out, felling Goths like ripe wheat, and rode back to our lines with the javelin still embedded in his skull, waving back and forth like some bizarre appendage. Our physicians later managed to extract it, but the wound turned bad and he died a few days later.

Another man named Arzes, one of Belisarius' Guards and a slight acquaintance of mine, also suffered a terrible wound. His men rescued him from the press, threw him over the back of a horse and escorted him back to the city for medical attention.

Our ranks parted to let them through, and I whistled between my teeth when I saw the Gothic arrow imbedded between his nose and right eye. An unusually skilled physician later managed to draw the arrow out and save Arzes's eye, by making an incision at the back of his neck and ripping the triple-pronged barb out through the hole. A grisly procedure, and one I was glad not to witness.

On the western side of the city, beyond my sight and hearing, our troops under Valerian and Martinus initially performed wonders. Their cavalry fell on the Gothic camps and threw them into confusion, slaughtering hundreds of their warriors and retreating in good order when reinforcements came storming up. Meantime the Roman citizen levies and their Moorish auxiliaries stayed quiet and motionless in the rear, where they could be most effective simply by looking formidable.

Procopius witnessed the battle on the Plains of Nero from the safety of the walls, and later that evening gave me a full account of the disaster that ensued.

"You may blame the Romans," he said, "for acting like fools instead of cowards. I think I preferred the latter. Seeing the Goths west of the river being thrown into disorder and routed by our cavalry, they abandoned all notions of discipline and poured forward, ignoring the shouts of their captains."

He paused to take a sip of wine and stare bleakly into our camp-fire. "Like all soldiers with the minimum of training, they forgot about the enemy and started to plunder the camps. The Goths, under Vitiges, rallied and counter-attacked. Our cavalry tried to stop them, but were engulfed and smashed to pieces. You should have seen Vitiges, Coel. He was like some pagan god of war, huge and terrible in his winged helm, his eyes flashing fire and brimstone. His sword was lightning in his hand, striking one man down after the other – stab-stab-stab! Alaric himself could have scarcely looked more terrible."

"If you have finished glorifying the enemy, what happened then?" I asked impatiently. Some of my Isaurians were seated in a circle around the fire and leaning forward intently, open-mouthed and wide-eyed, to catch his words. They loved stories, and Procopius loved an audience, so the two were well suited.

"The Romans broke and fled," he said with a shrug, slightly nettled by my directness, "and were pursued all the way back to Rome. Hundreds died before they reached the safety of the gates. There will be a great many widows and orphans weeping over their lost menfolk tonight. Our surviving cavalry would have been destroyed to a man, if not for the arrival of Bochas."

Bochas was one of the officers Belisarius had placed in command of his cavalry. When news of the unfolding disaster in the Plains of Nero reached the general, he had recalled as many men as he could from the fighting beside the Tiber and sent them to relieve Valerius and Martinus.

The collapse of our army on the Plains of Nero, precipitated by the ill-timed charge of the Romans, occurred at the same time as Belisarius' attack to the north started to falter. The Goths had poured more men into the battle, replacing their earlier losses, and after hours of fighting our cavalry were tiring and running short of arrows.

Belisarius was not fool enough, thank God, to commit his infantry to try and rescue the situation. We remained at our posts, watching our horse-archers fight with the utmost skill and bravery. Time and again, they charged into endless clouds of arrows, before wheeling, retreating, splitting up and reforming for another assault.

The Goths bided their time. When the sun hovered low on the horizon, and the reeking plain was bathed in red-gold light, the droning of their horns swept the field. This was the signal for fresh squadrons of Gothic and Frankish cavalry, held in reserve until now, to burst from the depleted lines of their infantry and charge our exhausted horsemen.

"Form line!" The order passed through our ranks and was taken up by each officer in turn, myself included.

The ground shook underfoot as my Isaurians formed into two lines of fifty, the last man on each flank almost rubbing shoulders with the men of the next squadron. They may have been a sullen and recalcitrant lot, but they knew their trade, and shuffled calmly into position.

As they were drilled, the front rank stood with their large round shields forming an interlocking wall, spears presented horizontally at chest height. Behind them the men of the rear rank stood with spears held upright, ready to step forward and fill any gaps in the line if we suffered casualties.

I stood behind them, just to the left of the rearmost man on the end of the line, watching in horror as the broken remains of our cavalry fled back towards the city. The Goths pursued relentlessly, spearing and chopping down the fugitives. In a moment, a few short seconds, the barbarian tide would roll over us.

"Ready!"

The order came from our captains of foot-archers. Again these were mostly Isaurians, formed up behind the lines of spearmen. A tremor passed through our army, accompanied by audible moans of fear, but the presence of the general steadied us.

"Stretch!"

Christ save us! They were less than twenty feet away now, a surging tide of galloping horses and gleaming lances and fierce, pale faces, hundreds of pairs of eyes blazing with hatred under bright steel helms.

It was death to stand firm against that charging horror. It was death to turn and run. I stood, fixed to the spot like a worm on a nail, my right hand curled tightly about Caledfwlch's hilt, as if my little sword would be of any use now.

"Loose!"

A rushing sound, like thousands of birds taking to the air at once, briefly drowned out the thunder of hoofs and the frantic hammering of my pulse.

The front rank of Gothic horsemen seemed to falter, their beasts twisting and rearing and screaming and plunging back onto their haunches. Their yelling riders were thrown, or shot from the saddle, and fell under the churning hoofs of the riders in the second line.

"Loose!"

A second flight of arrows, darkening the skies, and a third, and a fourth, pouring like hail into the Gothics, mowing down riders and horses and throwing their ranks into desperate confusion.

"At them!" screamed one of my Isaurians, "kill them all! Just kill them!"

He would have broken ranks and rushed forward, taking others with him, but I seized his shoulder and dragged him back into line.

"Stand your ground, fool!" I hissed into his ear, "or I'll have your skin flayed off your back and made into a sword-belt!"

He grinned at my threat, which wasn't quite the reaction I wanted, but at least he obeyed, and the line held firm.

Our trumpets sounded from the walls, signaling the retreat. Belisarius had no intention of trying to rescue the battle now. He merely aimed to withdraw in good order and get the remnants of the army back inside Rome.

Executing a fighting retreat is one of the most difficult manoeuvres, especially with darkness falling and terror pounding through your veins, the screams of dying men and beasts sounding in your ears, the stench of death curdling in your nostrils, and you're so frightened and deafened you can barely think or hear or speak.

My Isaurians were up to the task. I barked at them to keep the line straight as they withdrew, spears presented to the enemy, but they would have easily done so without me. Step by step, calmly and unhurriedly, they moved back towards the Salarian Gate. Our retreat was covered by the archers, who continued to shoot until the Goths, sickened by the casualties they had suffered, turned and fell back.

They left a great pile of wreckage on the field, human and animal, wounded beasts thrashing and screaming in their death-throes, men trying to crawl back to their own lines, or simply flopping down to die. Isaurian mountain men are superb archers, as good as any Huns or Scythians, and not to be despised as mere infantry.

We got back inside, along with the rest of the infantry and surviving cavalry, and the gates slammed shut before the Goths could regroup and pursue.

Procopius left our fire just before midnight, having exhausted his fund of stories. Most of my Isaurians had taken themselves to bed, weary but not dispirited by the defeat, for none of them had died. Our cavalry had suffered, true, but so had the Goths, and Rome was still secure.

I sat up late with a few men around the flickering embers of the fire, brooding over the conduct of the Romans. If not for their arrogant stupidity, we would not have lost so many men in a futile and pointless sally, and Belisarius' record would not bear the stain of a defeat, only the second he had ever suffered in the field.

The hour was extremely late, and I was drowsing alone over a final cup of wine, when I heard a commotion. I looked up, blinking in the sudden harsh glow of torch-light, and saw Photius sneering down at me.

He was as luminously handsome as ever, and his breastplate polished to a shine that hurt the eyes. He held a spatha in his right hand, and leveled the keen blade at my throat.

A dozen guardsmen stood behind him, tall and forbidding in their cloaks and crested helms. I glanced at their grim faces, silhouetted by the light of the torches they held, and my heart fell.

"Coel the Briton," said Photius in a gloating voice, "you are under arrest."

20.

The plot my enemies had hatched against me was a squalid one. Frustrated in their efforts to have me murdered, they changed their strategy, and tried to have me disgraced and condemned to death on a false charge of theft.

You might wonder why, as I did, that Photius' mother did not simply kill me when I lay for three days and nights in her power. I mulled over this as Photius and his men escorted me through the streets towards Belisarius' house on the Pincian Hill.

They had taken Caledfwlch – I thought it folly to try and fight so many, knowing that Photius would cheerfully allow his men to kill me for resisting arrest – and snapped heavy manacles on my wrists. I was used to this sort of treatment, having been exposed to it in Constantinople, and tried to keep my mind clear.

"You are a great fool, Photius," I said to the tall, manly figure striding at the head of our little procession, "your mother is using you as a weapon. Why do you do it? There is no private quarrel between us."

He stopped, and I almost ran into him as he turned on his heel and glared at me with pure hatred in his eyes, teeth clenched, nostrils flared like a war-horse about to charge into battle.

"You may as well hold your tongue," he rasped, "for I will not listen to the lies that flow from it. I know well how you tried to ravish my lady mother in Carthage, and how she only slipped from your grasp thanks to the grace of God and the aid of a servant. Will you pretend that you are innocent, or have forgotten the incident, you rank barbarian dog? That you did not defile her flesh with your filthy hands?"

So that was it. I had suspected something of the kind. This Photius had inherited a share of Antonina's beauty, but not much of her brains, and had allowed himself to be manipulated into believing a clumsy lie.

"Your mother," I said, holding his gaze, "is a liar. Her servant invited me to the palace in Carthage on a false pretext. Antonina tried to seduce me there, to discredit me in the eyes of Belisarius. I refused her. No doubt she has spun you a very different tale, but mine is the truth."

He gave a wordless cry and backhanded me across the face, cutting the skin with the large silver ring on his middle finger. I was rocked back on my heels, but saved from falling by the guardsmen holding my arms.

"She warned me you would try and talk your way out of it," he hissed, shoving his face close to mine, so close I could smell the odour of wine and spices on his breath, "but we have no secrets, my mother and I."

I could have laughed at that. Antonina was a sly and subtle creature, a snake in lovely human form, and harboured more secrets in her breast than this bone-headed youth could possibly imagine. However, there seemed little point in provoking him further, so I held back.

"What, then?" I asked, trying not to flinch at the feel of warm blood trickling down my cheek, "on what pretext do you arrest me? I presumed you mean to have me put on trial. Belisarius will require a full explanation."

He grinned, white teeth flashing in the gloom, and turned to one of his soldiers. "This man is a thief, is that not correct?" he asked.

"Yes, sir," the man replied, "we found these on his person."

He reached inside the folds of his cloak and produced a pair of ceremonial daggers made of pure gold. Beautiful objects, with smooth curving hilts and leaf-shaped blades. I had never set eyes on them before, and said so.

"Another lie," said Photius, clucking his tongue, "are all you Britons so deceitful? You stole these daggers from Presidius, seven days ago."

I had to think to match the name to a face. Then it came to me. Presidius was an Italian nobleman, a native of Spoleto who volunteered to join our army when Constantine took that city from the Goths.

He was said to have fallen under the displeasure of the Gothic monarch, and had only thrown in his lot with us to avoid punishment. I knew he was unpopular, and had acquired a reputation for being proud and haughty, overbearing to the lower orders and incompetent in the field.

"Presidius was a rich man, once," Photius added, "but when our men fled Spoleto he was obliged to leave most of his treasures behind, bar a few trinkets. These daggers are by far the most valuable of his possessions. And you stole them."

I found it difficult to keep the contempt from my voice. "First, you try and murder me on the battlefield," I said, "then your mother sends a pair of assassins after me. By the way, I slew the guardsman you bribed, and his body lies rotting under the ground by Naples. Now you stoop to having me framed on a false charge of petty theft. For shame, Photius. Don't you feel the slightest bit ashamed? Does that noble exterior of yours not contain a sliver of conscience?"

His face flooded with colour, but I carried on regardless. "If you were any sort of a man, which you're not, you would order your men to remove the chains on my wrists. Then we could have it out, man to man, blade to blade, and let God decide the victor. Or are you afraid to fight me?"

This was my last – my only – throw of the dice. If Photius possessed any sense of honour, which was doubtful, he could not refuse a fair challenge to trial by combat in front of his men. Whether I could beat this active young soldier, all muscle and sinew and whipcord, was another matter, but death in combat was preferable to disgrace and execution.

Sadly, my initial judgment of his character proved correct. "Vermin such as you don't deserve an honourable death," he hissed, "why should I, a Roman of noble blood, consent to cross swords with a felon?"

He turned on his heel before I could taunt him any further, and we continued on our way to the Pincian Hill.

I could scarcely believe that Photius meant to drag me in front of Belisarius, just hours after our army had suffered a defeat, but there was method in his eagerness. Tired and dispirited after the day's fighting, Belisarius might be vulnerable, and sufficiently disorientated to treat the absurd charges against me seriously instead of dismissing them out of hand.

A sound strategy, devised by someone who knew the workings of the general's mind: Antonina, no doubt. Only now did I realise the full breadth of her spite. Merely killing me wasn't enough, else she might have done it while I lay helpless under her knife. I had to be exposed as a thief and a traitor, my reputation torn to shreds in public, before my body was consigned to the gallows. Only then would her desire for revenge (and Theodora's) be sated.

I wondered if Presidius was part of the plot, or just a useful straw man to set up against me. When we reached Belisarius' house, still blazing with light despite the lateness of the hour, I saw him waiting outside with a couple of Persian bodyguards. He was a balding, pot-bellied man, greasy of countenance and character, and avoided my eyes as the guards shoved me up the steps.

"Whatever they paid you," I called out to him, "will not be enough to clear the taint from your soul if you give evidence against me. You know I did not steal your daggers, Presidius."

He sniffed and looked away, fluttering his fat fingers. I would get no help from that quarter. Antonina had bought his loyalty, and she had sufficient gold and silver to drown any man's conscience.

The hall glowed with light from rows of torches burning in sconces in the walls. Belisarius and his captains were poring over a great pile of maps laid out on a table. Their armour was still smeared with blood and mud from the battle, and their competing voices had a faintly hysterical edge.

Antonina had no business being present at a council of war, but a couch had been set up for her beside her husband's chair. She lounged on it, eyes half-closed, a faint smile playing on her lips as she listened to the men argue.

Her husband's face resembled a death's head. His eyes were hollow with exhaustion, skin yellow as old parchment, hand shaking as he stabbed at various points on a map of Rome. Sheer pride and strength of will were the only things holding him upright, and his voice quavered as it strained to be heard over the babble of his officers.

Their voices died away when Photius announced our presence by stamping his feet and raising his hand in salute. His mother's eyes snapped open, and she sat upright on her couch. Curse the woman, but I believe she actually winked at me.

"Photius," said Belisarius, rubbing his bristly jaw, his tired eyes flicking between me and my captors, "what is this? Why have you brought the faithful Coel here, loaded down with chains?"

"It gives me no joy to be here," replied Photius, still standing stiffly to attention, "but there is one who can explain better than me."

Presidius shuffled into the hall, followed by his Persian guards. They were big, striking men, with oiled and plaited beards and ornate armour, and wore curved scimitars at their hips. Hired, no doubt, with some of the tainted gold Antonina had tipped into his purse.

"Sir," he trilled, mopping his sweating chops with a plump hand, "it grieves me to inform you that this officer, Coel, has brought disgrace upon himself and the honour of Roman arms. Seven nights since, as I lay asleep in my quarters, I saw him steal into my bedchamber and remove a pair of golden daggers from my chest. The daggers were virtually all that remained of my fortune, the majority of which, as you know, I had to leave behind in Spoleto."

The guardsman carrying the daggers stepped forward and produced them with a flourish from inside his cloak, holding them up for all to see.

Belisarius screwed his eyes shut and rubbed his face, clearly struggling to comprehend this fresh and unwelcome development.

"For God's sake," he muttered, "as if we did not have enough to occupy our time. Photius, could you not have waited until tomorrow before bringing this to my attention?"

"I am sorry, sir," Photius replied smartly, "but I felt the matter was best deal with quickly. The dishonourable and criminal conduct of this officer casts shame on us all."

Belisarius looked to his officers for help. Bessas and Troglita were dumbfounded, but Constantine appeared to be in the grip of a fever. He held onto the table for support, his face grey and drained of colour. I have already hinted at what an emotional and unstable man he was, ruled by his passions, and how he regarded me with something like hero-worship for rescuing him at Membresa. Now he was exposed to the sight of his idol, stripped of honour and dignity and charged with a crime abominable in its vulgarity. Theft! Any Roman officer worth his salt would open his veins before even thinking of committing such a low act.

To do him credit, though it worked against me in this instance, Belisarius never shirked his duty. As commander-in-chief and de factor governor of Rome, he was responsible for dispensing justice, and obliged to hold a court-martial.

He wearily ordered the table to be cleared away, and held the trial there and then, seated as chief justice with Bessas and Troglita as subordinates. A slave was sent to rouse Procopius from his bedchamber next to the general's quarters, to act in my defence.

The secretary came, grumbling and rubbing his eyes, and looked startled at the scene laid out before him. Just a few short hours ago, we had been sitting and prosing around a camp-fire, and now here I was on trial for my life.

"Coel," said Belisarius when I was brought before his chair, "this is a grave matter. Have you anything to say?"

"Just this," I replied, looking him square in the eye, "the charges against me are patently false. You know me, sir, and that I have never looked for private gain. I have very little in this world, but that little contents me. The notion that I would steal into another officer's bedchamber and take his possessions is absurd."

Procopius loudly cleared his throat and looked to Belisarius for permission to speak. It was granted with a nod from the chair, and he turned to fix Presidius with a malicious eye.

"Are we to believe," he said, speaking slowly and clearly, every word dripping with sarcasm, "that Coel, a fine officer who has done nothing but distinguish himself in the service of Rome, decided to implicate himself in such a clumsy and foolish crime? And that Presidius" – here he stabbed an accusing finger at the quaking Italian – "simply lay there in bed as the thief went about his work, too frightened to challenge him or raise the alarm? Would not a soldier of Rome, even such a mediocre one as this, have made some attempt to defend his property?"

Presidius nervously rubbed his hands, and attempted to summon up the ghost of his old arrogance.

"My courage is not on trial here," he squeaked, "I was somewhat mazed with drink, and the sudden appearance of the thief surprised me. He was gone almost before I could speak."

"Ah!" Procopius clasped his hands. "You were the worse for wine. So drunk, in fact, you neglected to lock and bar your door before retiring?"

Presidius gave a nervous little jerk of his head, and replied this was so.

"And you are certain the thief was Coel?" Procopius pressed, "mazed, as you put it, with drink, you were able to see him?"

"I keep a candle burning through the night," replied the other, his voice unsteady and thick with deceit, "the light fell across Coel's face as he ran from the room. I am certain, beyond a shred of doubt, that it was him."

Procopius paused for a moment, frowning and pulling at his lower lip. "Seven days," he said at last, "you waited seven days before bringing this charge against the accused. Why wait?"

"Rome was under threat, and every man was needed to meet the Goths in the field. I did not wish to harm our cause with an unnecessary distraction."

It was feeble stuff, and I could see Procopius champing at the bit to tear Presidius's story to shreds, but now Photius intervened.

"Consider, sirs," he said, "Coel is a poor man, and getting on in years. Despite his fine record of service, he is still unmarried and childless, with no property and no money save his soldier's wage. His only possession is an old sword of little value beyond the sentimental. He sees a brother officer, a lesser man than he in terms of merit and ability, but possessed of wealth in the form of two golden daggers."

He snapped his fingers. "Something breaks under the strain of envy and greed. He casts aside his honour, the honour that has brought him nothing save a couple of minor promotions and a host of old wounds, and stoops to base robbery. Presidius came to speak with me earlier this evening. Acting on his information, we arrested Coel and found the daggers on his person."

"Liar!" I shouted, goaded beyond measure, but his guards hauled me back. My fingers convulsed, aching to wrap around his throat.

Belisarius didn't know what to make of it. He might have thrown out the charge of theft as ridiculous and ill-founded, if not for the involvement of Photius. Once again, Antonina proved to be the blind spot in his judgment. For his darling wife's sake, he had always looked on her son with affection, and struggled to believe that he would willingly participate in some crude plot against a fellow officer.

The general drew himself up. "This affair shall be deferred until tomorrow evening," he said, "for now, we have far more pressing matters to attend to. Until then, the daggers shall be restored to their owner, and Coel shall be confined to barracks."

I felt relieved at his judgment. Deferring the trial until the next day, when he was refreshed and could think clearly, was just the respite I had hoped for. Viewed in the cold and unforgiving light of day, the case against me would seem even more flimsy.

Constantine, the fool, chose this moment to intervene. "This trial is a sham," he declared, stepping between me and Belisarius, "and I can prove it with my own testimony."

"Be silent, man," snapped Bessas, but Constantine ignored him.

"Presidius is mistaken," he said, "for it was not Coel who stole into his chamber and took the daggers. It was me."

A stunned silence fell over the hall. I stared at Constantine, and for a second wondered if he had run mad. Then the truth dawned: he was sacrificing himself on my behalf, as payment for rescuing him. He had often promised to clear the debt between us, in spite of my protests, and here was his opportunity.

To my eternal shame, I let him do it. I opened my mouth to deny his testimony, but the words stuck in my throat. Survival was all, and my instinct for self-preservation proved stronger than my sense of honour.

The affair was now clearly beyond Belisarius. He gaped like a landed fish at Constantine, raised his hands, and lowered them again. Photius and Presidius were at a total loss – this wasn't part of their scheme – and Antonina's face was a mask of barely concealed fury. Seeing her so distraught went a little way to compensating for my shame.

The game was slipping away from her, but she was not quite swept from the board. With a rustle of silks, she rose from her couch and approached Belisarius' chair.

"A crime has been committed," she said, resting a pale hand, glimmering with silver rings, on her husband's shoulder, "it is your duty to see that justice is done, and the offender punished. Whoever he may be."

Her eyes briefly met mine. There was no patronising mockery in them now, just sheer hatred burning like twin flames in the depths of her irises.

For once, Belisarius resisted her will. "I make no judgments tonight," he said, gently patting her hand, "we must have more time to consider the facts. It is a complex case, and Coel deserves a fair trial."

Constantine panicked. "No!" he shouted, "we will have a judgment now!"

God help me, he drew his sword and rushed at Belisarius. The general's instincts saved him. He threw himself sideways out of his chair – a half-second earlier, and the blade would have plunged into his heart.

The whole incident lasted mere seconds, but is engraved on my memory in a sequence of tableaus, like friezes carved from stone. Bessas and Troglita leaped on Constantine and bore him to the ground. His sword clattered on the tiles as it was wrenched from his grip.

Panting, but unhurt, Belisarius got to his feet, gesturing at his wife to stand back. She looked genuinely frightened, though whether from concern for his well-being, or the loss of prestige she would suffer if he died, I could not tell. Events had now spiraled beyond her control, and she was incapable of wresting back the initiative.

Or so I thought. For assaulting a superior officer with intent to kill, Constantine had condemned himself to death. It was a split-second decision, and perhaps by doing so he hoped to absolve me completely. Certainly, the focus was now on him.

He was entitled to a trial, just as I was. While Bessas and Troglita held Constantine down, Antonina took her husband to one side and spoke urgently to him. I cast a hopeless glance at Procopius, who looked solemn and gave a little shake of his head, as if warning me not to do or say anything unwise.

When Antonina had finished, Belisarius stood still and silent for a moment, staring bleakly at the floor. Then he raised his hand and summoned two of his guards. They were half-hidden in the shadows to the rear of the hall, and I had failed to see them until now.

"Take that man to a side-room," he said, pointing at Constantine, "and strangle him."

21.

Constantine's death was my salvation. Unwilling to risk any more scandal, Belisarius refused to credit the charges against me, or to listen to any more pleas from Photius and Presidius. He dismissed us all, and gave orders that for the time being I should stay in Procopius' quarters, with a guard on the door. The golden daggers were restored to Presidius, who had never really lost them, and Caledfwlch to my keeping.

The execution without trial of Constantine cast a long shadow over Belisarius' reputation. All the suspicions that he was a pawn of his wife, easily manipulated by her – and through her, by the Empress – were confirmed, and for a time he lost the respect of his captains. Only his record of virtually unbroken military success, and his enduring popularity among the men, saved him from being ousted. Bessas, for one, never quite held Belisarius in the same high regard again, though he continued to serve under him.

Ridden with guilt, for I knew that my failure to speak at the right time had helped to damn Constantine, I was escorted to Procopius's quarters and given a bed in an antechamber.

There I remained for three days, sweating on my fate. Procopius was absent for most of the time, being required to attend on Belisarius. When he returned, usually late at night, he was tired but polite enough, though the old intimacy that had existed between us was gone. I had become a dangerous man to know, too dangerous even for him, and the shadow of the noose hung over my head.

On the third evening of my confinement Procopius returned with four of Belisarius' guards at his back, and summoned me to the general's presence.

"What is to become of me?" I asked, rising. Procopius looked grim, and the guards regarded me with hostile eyes, as though I was responsible for their master's shame.

"You will find out soon enough," the secretary replied curtly.

We trooped down the shadowy corridor to Belisarius' own bedchamber, which had six guards on the door instead of the usual two. Evidently he felt threatened, and feared that erstwhile comrades might make an attempt on his life. I gave a wry smile. Now Belisarius knew how I felt all the time.

We entered to find him in his nightgown and perched in a window seat overlooking the northern walls of Rome. Hundreds of lights glimmered in the darkness beyond, the campfires of the Gothic army.

He turned from his vigil to regard us somberly, hands folded behind his back, like a disapproving schoolmaster.

"My wife is not here," he said without greeting or preamble, "I have decided to send her to Naples, and she and her ladies are preparing for the journey. She will be safer there, and can wait out the rest of the war in peace."

"You will be glad of that," he said, nodding at me, "I know now that Antonina is no friend of yours. It pains me to discover the enmity between my wife and one of my best officers. Despite that, you are also going to Naples."

I stood silent, waiting patiently for an explanation. Unless he had run mad, presumably he did not mean to send myself and Antonina off together.

Belisarius turned back to the latticed window. "Look at that," he murmured, indicating the Gothic fires, "they are inexhaustible. No matter how many of the barbarians we kill, fresh men spring up from the earth to replace them. All the while our numbers dwindle, and our supplies run low. Did you know the citizens have started to eat grass, Coel?"

The question startled me. "I had heard something, sir," I replied unsteadily, "but witnessed nothing of the sort."

"It is true," he said, nodding sadly, "the poor are reduced to eating herbs and grasses, and eating the flesh of mules. The meat is tainted, since the animals died of disease, and now a pestilence is sweeping through the poor quarters of Rome. I have ordered fresh corn to be distributed, but there isn't enough to feed all. My physicians do what they can, but nothing can stop the sickness from spreading."

He ran his hands down his bearded cheeks. "God forgive us. What misery and destruction we have brought to this city. All for some vain, foolish dream of restoring the glory of the Western Empire. Glory! What glory? We have brought nothing but death. No, do not absolve your guilt by blaming mere soldiers, who must follow orders and do their duty. I, Belisarius, have brought nothing but death. Yet I must perform my own duty, and see the game through to the end."

I had never heard Belisarius speak his heart so honestly. He seemed to have forgotten our presence, and looked up with a start when Procopius gave a discreet little cough.

"Coel," said Belisarius, "our poor, persecuted Briton. You must have often cursed the day your mother fled your homeland and came halfway across the world to find refuge in Constantinople. Some refuge. It is a miracle you are still alive, but I must ask you to perform another duty. You will leave Rome, tonight, in the company of Procopius, and make your way through the Gothic lines. Once you reach Naples, you will send out orders for our garrisons scattered about Campania to send part of their men to muster at the city."

"We must have reinforcements," he said, leaning forward to stare intently at me, "if the Emperor sends none, then I have no choice but to weaken our garrisons elsewhere. You will handle the military aspect of the mission. Procopius is tasked with devising some way of getting provisions into the city from the south. Our stores of corn will soon be expended. Without fresh supplies, the Romans may soon revert to even older practices than the worship of pagan gods, and start eating each other."

The quest was a daunting one, with much risk involved, but at least the shadow of execution had lifted. Whether Belisarius wanted me out of the city just to perform a useful service, or because my presence was an embarrassment to him, I could not be certain. Whatever his motives, I was grateful to go.

I had one question. "What of Photius, sir? Is he to accompany his mother to Naples?"

Belisarius gazed at me for a full minute before replying. "No. He stays here."

Where I can keep my eye on him, he might have added, but I didn't press the issue. Antonina's scheming son would remain stranded in Rome, where I sincerely hoped he might catch a Gothic arrow in his throat before too much longer. Meanwhile I was being given an opportunity to escape well beyond his reach.

Procopius and I, along with six Huns as an escort, left the city soon after midnight via the gate of Saint Paul. This gate was located at the beginning of the road that connected Rome to Ostia, the fortified coastal town that the Goths had seized shortly after the beginning of the siege.

It was a black, moonless night, and we departed like thieves, clad in dark cloaks and mantles and with mufflers wrapped around our horses' hoofs.

At first we led the beasts on foot, wishing to spare them in case we needed to escape pursuit later. The lights of the Gothic camp were at their fewest here, since they already held Ostia and there was no possible escape for us in that direction.

Besides the Huns, Belisarius had also given us a scout, a native of Rome, to guide our way. We had no lanterns, for that would have alerted the Gothic pickets, but our guide seemed able to find his way in the dark.

I recall he somewhat resembled a sniffer hound, being short and bow-legged, and with a raddled, jowly, somewhat collapsed face. He said little, and responded to Procopius's frantically whispered questions with curt grunts.

Procopius was understandably frightened, even though he had some experience in this kind of secret work. The Goths and their allies were all around us, and it seemed an impossible task to pick a safe path through their teeming lines.

The guide led us half a mile beyond the gate, and then abruptly swung south, straight towards the fortified Gothic camp established to keep watch over the Appian Way. Beyond the camp lay the dark mass of the broken aqueducts that Vitiges had ordered repaired and filled with soldiers.

"Be ready to ride," was all the guide would say. Procopius gave up trying to get anything more out of him, and the eight of us followed in silence.

The walls of Rome were to our right, illuminated by the glow of torches and braziers on the walls. I wondered if the more sharp-eyed of our sentries might see us, and prayed fervently they wouldn't call out a challenge or raise the alarm, thinking we were a band of Goths trying to sneak into the city.

At any moment I dreaded encountering some of the mounted scouts that scoured the countryside around Rome. It was unlikely that any would be abroad at such an hour, but my fears multiplied as we plodded over the flat, open ground west of Rome. The darkness was our friend, but still I perspired freely, imagining a sudden shower of arrows and javelins, followed by hordes of Gothic pony-soldiers.

Incredibly, our little Italian guide led us safely through the enemy outposts. He knew the lay of the land intimately, and led us on clever detours, using whatever scraps of cover were available and steering clear of the scattered watch-fires.

I like to think we moved swiftly and silently, like ghosts, and we did make all speed, but were also aided by the Gothic habit of drinking themselves into a stupor. Confident after their recent victory, convinced that the Romans would not dare attempt another sally, their rough discipline had almost fallen away completely. We crept past groups of bearded soldiers singing in loud, drunken voices and downing cup after cup of their glutinous ale, when they should have been keeping watch.

We passed almost directly under the timber stockade of their camp. The sentries must have been blind, or every bit as drunk as their comrades, and we crept past unchallenged.

"The barbarians have grown complacent," whispered Procopius, "Belisarius might ride out now, and slaughter them as they lie swine-drunk beside their fires."

Then we came to the aqueducts. The Goths had walled up the lower arches where they met, between the Latin and Appian Ways, and stationed the majority of their garrison there. Our guide took us west, until our feet were treading the smooth, ancient flagstones of the Appian Way. In their arrogance the Goths had thought to place few pickets here, so far from Rome and deep inside their own lines.

Only once did we encounter danger. A single watch-fire burned under the crumbling ruins of an arch at the extreme western end of one of the aqueducts, warming the bones of a trio of Gothic spearmen.

They were huddled up miserably against the cold, and seemed indifferent to anything except staying close to the guttering fire. We tried to pass by too quickly, and one of them tipped up his helmet and called out a challenge.

Procopius had studied the Gothic tongue, and barked a response. The Goth didn't seem satisfied. He rose to a sitting position, peering at us suspiciously as he clutched his spear.

"Mount," hissed our guide. I already had one leg hooked over the saddle, and within seconds we were forcing our horses into a gallop along the highway. We kept them at a fast pace until the rugged silhouette of the aqueducts were a distant line on the horizon. There was no pursuit: either the sentry failed to raise the alarm, or his superiors failed to heed him.

Naples was almost two days' ride away. We covered a portion of the distance that night, and rested at dawn, sinking to sleep inside a little grove just as the sun broke cover in the east.

We were inside the borders of Campania, and practically clear of danger, for the Goths had concentrated their forces around Rome and in the north of Italy. Thanks to the earlier conquests of Belisarius, Campania was imperial territory, and would remain so unless Rome fell and Vitiges could push his armies south.

Dusk of the second days' ride brought us within sight of the walls of Naples again, and the blue sparking waters of the bay.

Procopius was the first to spur his horse onto a ridge overlooking the city. He reined in and shaded his eyes, looking out to sea, and gave an excited yelp.

"Coel!" he shouted, beckoning at me. I rode up to join him, and looked down at the glorious spread of the city, white walls shining in the late afternoon sun, and the broad waters of the ocean beyond.

The sea was full of ships, bobbing at anchor in the bay. Transports, galleys and dromons, all with imperial flags fluttering from their mast-heads.

Every ship was packed with soldiers. The Emperor had not forgotten us after all, and sent thousands of troops to our aid.

More Books by David Pilling

The Half-Hanged Man
The White Hawk (I)
The White Hawk (II): Rebellion
The White Hawk (III): Restoration
Caesar's Sword (I): The Red Death
Caesar's Sword (II): Siege of Rome
Robin Hood (I)
Robin Hood (II): The Wrath of God
Robin Hood (III): The Hooded Man
Nowhere Was There Peace
The Best Weapon (with Martin Bolton)
Sorrow (with Martin Bolton)

The John Swale Chronicles
Folville's Law & 12 mini-sequels

Follow David at his blogs at:
Blogspot: pillingswritingcorner
Weebly: davidpillingauthor

Or contact him direct at:
Davidpilling56@hotmail.com

Printed in Great Britain
by Amazon